"When it comes to the n[...] does it better than Jonat[...] pulling back the curtain a[...] adults. In *Welcoming the F[...]* teach but to listen and re[...] [...], celebrating feedback, bringing energy, and playing Farkle are notions we can all consider and implement. (Although I would recommend Kan Jam over Farkle.) As a pastor and a father to young adults, I'm thankful for JP's wisdom."

Kyle Idleman, senior pastor of Southeast Christian Church
and author of *Not a Fan* and *Don't Give Up*

"In *Welcoming the Future Church*, you can learn from one of the greatest practitioners I have ever met who will prophetically remind you of truths that work, not only for the rising generations but for all people. Dive in and dedicate yourself to this book, and you will be welcomed to a more effective future ministry."

Todd Wagner, senior pastor of Watermark Community Church
and author of *Come and See*

"I believe in this generation rising up, using their gifts in a local church, and being unleashed into the world as a force for the kingdom of God. JP is watching the next generation come back to the church, and this book will help you engage in the same work."

Jennie Allen, author of *Nothing to Prove* and founder
and visionary of IF:Gathering

"Wow. JP has written a stellar book here. There isn't much more of a pressing issue than raising up faithful, Jesus-following, and Jesus-loving leaders of the next generation, but not many are equipping us or showing us how to do it like JP. I am grateful for this resource and the impact it will have on generations to come!"

Jefferson Bethke, *New York Times* bestselling author of *Jesus > Religion*

"I couldn't recommend this book more highly. I don't know a person alive who has more experience and expertise in leading and unleashing young adults to build the future of the church! This book is a resource today's church desperately needs to read and apply."

David Marvin, leader of The Porch

"*Welcoming the Future Church* is a must-read manifesto. As a leader in the trenches, JP helps us not only understand this generation but equips us in unlocking their potential for greater mission."

David Nasser, pastor, author, and university leader.

"This leader and these leadership principles changed my life forever and redirected my time, talent, and treasure to be leveraged whole-heartedly for God's kingdom. It has been the privilege of my life to have a front-row seat watching God's mighty work through JP in the lives of thousands of young adults."

Greg Crooks, executive pastor of Watermark Community Church

"Most content on the next generation is just research and statistics. But not this book. This is one of the most practical toolkits for engaging the next generation I have seen. It's a behind-the-scenes look at what made the largest young adult ministry in the nation what it is today. If you're a pastor considering next-gen engagement, it doesn't make sense not to read this."

Grant Skeldon, founder of Initiative Network

"Here is a resource that will compel you to replace fear with faith when contemplating the trajectory of Jesus's church. I trust this book because I trust the author. JP truly is one of the most godly, wise, passionate, and strategic leaders I know. I am so grateful that one of the most effective leaders of young adults has written a book on leading young adults."

Timothy Ateek, executive director of Breakaway Ministries

"If you want to learn and lead young adults, learn from and be led by JP. There is no greater leader, visionary, or mission-minded pastor of young adults than Jonathan Pokluda. God has gifted him with an understanding, a voice, and a heroic kingdom vision that is deploying the young adult population in world-changing ways. And now, from a desire to see the church flourish and Christ be exalted, he is giving that expertise and learning away to all in *Welcoming the Future Church*."

John Elmore, director of community and re:generation, Watermark Community Church

"At Passion, I have spent much of my life watching and influencing the up-and-coming generation. Over the years, I have learned so much from watching and knowing JP, and I believe that the wisdom of this book will help you be better positioned to help serve and lead the future church."

Brad Jones, Atlanta City pastor, Passion City Church

Welcoming the Future Church

HOW TO REACH, TEACH, AND ENGAGE YOUNG ADULTS

Jonathan "JP" Pokluda

with Luke Friesen

BakerBooks

a division of Baker Publishing Group
Grand Rapids, Michigan

© 2020 by Jonathan Pokluda

Published by Baker Books
a division of Baker Publishing Group
PO Box 6287, Grand Rapids, MI 49516-6287
www.bakerbooks.com

Printed in the United States of America

Library of Congress Cataloging-in-Publication Data
Names: Pokluda, Jonathan, 1980– author.
Title: Welcoming the future church : how to reach, teach, and engage young adults / Jonathan Pokluda, with Luke Friesen.
Description: Grand Rapids : Baker Books, a division of Baker Publishing Group, 2020.
Identifiers: LCCN 2019028427 | ISBN 9780801078118 (paperback)
Subjects: LCSH: Church work with young adults.
Classification: LCC BV4446 .P65 2020 | DDC 259/.25—dc23
LC record available at https://lccn.loc.gov/2019028427

20 21 22 23 24 25 26   7 6 5 4 3 2 1

To Todd Wagner:
thank you for your incredible investment in me.

To The Porch Team:
*we have been in the trenches together,
watching God change lives and partnering with him.*

Contents

Introduction

The World's Most Influential Generation

More than seventy million people watched a three-minute music video we made about Millennials. I wouldn't be surprised if you're one of them, but just in case you haven't seen it yet, search "Millennials by Micah Tyler" on YouTube.[1] Go ahead—watch it! I'll be right here.

I asked my friend Micah, who is a Millennial, to make that video to open a talk I gave at the Church Leaders Conference in 2016 about the importance of reaching young adults.[2] It's a catchy tune that parodies all kinds of Millennial stereotypes, from still living with their parents to essential oils to participation trophies and man buns. Um, ouch? Or at least some people felt that way. Reaction to the video was immediate, immense, and mixed. On Watermark Community Church's Facebook page alone, where the video was originally posted, it got more than nine million views, one hundred and fifty thousand shares, fifty thousand reactions, and nearly five thousand comments. Other sites and stations then picked it up, and it went completely viral, getting more than thirty million total views in the first week. One of the lines in the song is, "Criticism isn't easy for their ears," and it wasn't. Some people said the video was unkind, un-Christian, and überjudgmental. Some people called it hate speech. Others called it ageism. I'd say the reaction to the video exactly proved the point it was making. Of course, the video wasn't actually sincere criticism. We were just making fun of ourselves—before getting down to the serious business of talking about how the church can teach, engage, and deploy young adults.

But really, why did so many people watch this video, share it with their friends, and weigh in with their opinion about it? Because it resonated so deeply with them. It tapped into some chords of truth about this incredibly gifted generation that also feels incredibly misunderstood.

I believe some people in the church have contributed significantly to that misunderstanding. You know Millennials and the generations following them are literally the future—that truth is undeniable—but you aren't sure how to reach them. And if you're not reaching them, there is no future for your church. I'm not trying to be harsh here; it's really just a math problem. If young adults aren't joining and leading in your church, eventually your church will die. Or at the very least, it will miss out on an opportunity to impact and unleash the most influential generation the world has ever seen. I want to help make sure your church doesn't miss out on Millennials and the next generation of leaders.

I'm a Millennial myself, and I've spent the last ten-plus years of my life trying to figure out how to reach and unleash this seemingly elusive group. Some call them Generation Y, some call them Millennials, others just call them young adults or the "next generation." I will use all those terms interchangeably to address those ages nineteen to thirty-five. I had the humbling privilege of teaching and leading tens of thousands of them through a ministry called The Porch (www.theporch.live), and I saw that ministry grow from a weekly gathering of 150 people to one with more than forty thousand people hearing teaching every week laden with the gospel and Scripture.

Besides my own experiences as a young adult, including my own mistakes and failures to learn from, throughout my time in ministry I have also walked alongside and counseled literally thousands of other people in their twenties or early thirties. I've learned so much about what some do to succeed at this crossroads and how some fail. I've seen what works and what doesn't work, what brings happiness and what brings pain. I've had the opportunity to study the Scriptures and to be mentored by Bible experts older and wiser than I am, and I have seen how following (or ignoring) God's wisdom leads to very different outcomes in life.

In studying this generation, I'm studying myself. So much of what I read about Millennials resonates with me personally. I want to do everything in my power to help you reach them. These are the leaders of tomorrow (and today), and you must invest in them. If God has given me grace in learning anything along the way, I want to entrust it to you (2 Tim. 2:2).

There are two main reasons I'm so passionate about reaching this demographic.

1. Because it's me. When I was twenty-one, I stumbled into a church and sat in the back row, hung over and smelling like smoke. I began to wrestle with the reality of "Who is Jesus?" He saved me, came into my life, and changed everything. He gave me a greater obsession and passion than any of the addictions I had, which were numerous. He began to replace them by the power of the Holy Spirit, and he gave me a new reason for living. I want to help rescue others who are caught up in the same cycle of sin and hopelessness I was, changing both their "now" and their "forever."

2. Because it's strategic. If you want to change the world for the cause of Christ, you are going to need to reach this generation. Why? Because they are the most influential generation the world has ever seen. Here are a few statistics about Millennials:

- A full one-third of the world's population is Generation Y, making it the biggest generation in history.
- 96 percent believe they will do something great in their lives.
- 87 percent think the environment is their responsibility—they are "green."
- 81 percent have volunteered in the past year.
- 79 percent said they want to work for a company that cares about how it affects or contributes to society.
- 77 percent said "helping others" was among their chief motivations in life.
- 61 percent feel personally responsible for making a difference in the world.
- 60 percent voted in the 2012 US presidential election. This was the highest young voter turnout ever, and the 2016 election was similar.[3]

All is not well with this generation, though. Here are a few other, much more sobering, statistics:

- Their number one goal (81 percent) is to get rich; their number two goal (51 percent) is to get famous.
- 75 percent claim that they are "spiritual but not religious," meaning that they have no ties to anything other than "spirituality."
- 68 percent say there is more than one true way to interpret the teachings of their religion.
- 64 percent believe that sex outside of marriage is morally acceptable.
- 59 percent of Millennial Christians disconnect from church after age fifteen, either permanently or for an extended period of time.
- 50 percent believe that all people are eventually saved no matter what they do.
- 44 percent say they feel or have felt depressed.
- 10 percent have considered committing suicide.[4]

Young adults are influencers, and they want to make a difference. Many of them are misguided, but if they can be shown how to use their gifts to make a difference bigger than themselves, they will be the most powerful force you have ever seen unleashed in your church. I believe that to my core. But it will take time, patience, knowledge, and strategy on your part. They will come into your church thinking, *Look at me*, and you will have to direct them to use their influence to say, "No, look at Jesus." How can you do that? Let's dig in together.

SECTION ONE

Teach

CHAPTER 1

Be Real

I was a porn addict for more than a decade before I became a Christian. It completely owned me. It was a struggle every day. But honestly, it wasn't really a struggle—I just binged on it repetitively. When I became a Christian and understood grace, I got on a path to recovery. The Holy Spirit began to do an amazing work in my life, changing my obsessions and freeing me from my addictions. Today I walk in an incredible (and frankly, miraculous) amount of freedom from lust and pornography. But that doesn't mean I'm immune to it. In fact, not too long ago, after years of freedom, I gave in to temptation and looked at nudity online. A few days later I was scheduled to preach a message about living by the Spirit instead of the flesh. Let me tell you—things got real in a hurry.

Being real is about being you—being who you really are. And being honest about your imperfections. Millennials hate inauthenticity, and they can smell it from a mile away. I believe inauthenticity is the number one reason young adults are leaving the church—or never show up in the first place. They think church is a place where people put only their best foot forward, hide their issues and problems, talk about surface-level things, and pretend to have it all together for an hour or two before going back to their normal, uninspired, no-different-from-anyone-else lives.

I wouldn't want to be a part of that either! I believe "being real" needs to affect at least two main areas of our lives: living out who we really are (not trying to be like someone else) and dealing with our sin transparently. This is so important. We must let this hit our heart. This needs to change how we do what we do.

I can remember when I realized the most strategic thing I could do with my life was to influence young adults to know Jesus. I did what so many of you have probably done. I started to audit who I thought was best reaching them, and I started listening to those people. I tried to preach like them. I caught myself saying things I had heard them say, even if it wasn't relevant to me. At the time, The Village Church was a young church, reaching young adults, and Watermark was a church born out of a young adult ministry.

One day I was driving down the road with a pastor-friend and reflecting on what I wanted to do with my life. I asked him, "What do you think I need to do to be the next Todd Wagner or Matt Chandler?" (the pastors of those two churches). He responded, "Let's start with, why do you want to be those guys? I think that would be a huge mistake." His point was clear. God made them who they are, and he made me who I am. I needed to be faithful with the story, gifts, and ministry God had entrusted to me and not try to be someone else.

Know Who You Are, Be Who You Are, Like Who You Are

Young adults don't want to follow a replica of your favorite celebrity pastor. If that's what you're trying to be, they won't follow you or even listen to what you're saying. They want to follow someone who is earnestly and sincerely following Christ. And you need to follow Christ by knowing who you are, being who you are, and liking who you are. This is real and attractive to young adults. They resonate with this kind of authentic living.

Know Who You Are

You are "fearfully and wonderfully made" (Ps. 139:14)! God didn't make a mistake when he put you together and gave you the personality, strengths, weaknesses, and experiences that make you who you are. Do you know what part of the body of Christ you are (1 Cor. 12:12–27)? There's a big difference between a foot, an ear, and a mouth. Can you articulate your strengths and spiritual gifts? Capitalize on those. Do you have a death grip on your weaknesses and a sober-minded knowledge of where Satan would first try to take you out? Focus on defending those areas. If *you* don't know who you really are, you won't be able to lead young adults into discovering who *they* really are and who they were meant to be. If you're not sure about your answers to those questions, ask those folks around you who know you well. Beg them for a no-holds-barred, biblically based assessment of your character, strengths, and weaknesses. You might not like everything they tell you, but you'll grow from it. (We'll talk more about feedback in a later chapter.)

Be Who You Are

You don't have to be hip and cool, wear skinny jeans, be tatted up, have a trendy hairstyle, or garner a million Instagram followers for young adults to listen to you. You just need to be you, toiling with them for the sake of the gospel and teaching them the Scriptures, and they will listen. Don't believe me? Just look at John Piper. I know many young adults have been impacted by his ministry. Is that guy hip? More like hip replacement. But the brother knows the Word, and it *bleeds* out of him. If you're cut, you should bleed Bible too. Being rooted in God's Word and in your identity in Christ will give you the confidence to live out the unique identity and personality he's given you. Young adults don't need you to be like them, but they need you to authentically be who God made you to be. You are God's man or woman, sovereignly placed exactly where he wants you (Acts 17:26) to be his ambassador (2 Cor. 5:20). He doesn't want or need you to be a clone of one of his other creations. We'll talk later about what it means to hold certain traditions loosely—since you probably could tweak some things about yourself or your strategy to reach young adults more effectively—but not at the expense of authenticity. Be yourself. That may not earn you a Piper-esque following, but it will ensure anyone following you is getting the real deal.

Like Who You Are

You need to enjoy who God made you to be! This might be the hardest one of them all. Do you like yourself, or do you wish you were more like somebody else? Do you embrace your part in the body of Christ, or are you a foot desperately trying to be a hand, or maybe a hand desperately trying to be a mouth? It's often dissatisfaction with ourselves that turns us into chameleons who want to be like others. This doesn't mean you shouldn't work on your weaknesses, or try to learn new things, or maybe even try to make your teaching more engaging. But it does mean you need to do business with the pride and envy that might be lurking in your heart and festering into a dislike of yourself. Comparing yourself with others will steal your joy. Desperately wanting to be liked, especially without truly liking yourself, will come across as a neediness that actually repulses young adults. But Christ-centered confidence is attractive!

Does this all sound like a tall order? Good. It is! Thankfully, you're not alone in this. "[God's] grace is sufficient for you, for [his] power is made perfect in weakness" (2 Cor. 12:9). To remind myself of this, I reflect on this thought nearly every day: *If dependence is the goal, then weakness is the advantage.* If dependence on God is the goal for me, then my many weaknesses are to my advantage. If I believe at my core I can't do anything without him, then these weaknesses push me into a deeper relationship with God. If you rely on the Lord to help you live authentically, knowing you are powerless to do so apart from his power working in you (John 15:5), that's exactly where you need to be.

Your Mess Becomes Your Message

Remember the porn addiction and recent slipup I mentioned? Here's what happened. Not too long ago, I was reading a friend's post on social media and clicked on a hashtag. It was an innocent hashtag, but it took me to another hashtag. That one wasn't so innocent. I clicked on it anyway. I knew I shouldn't have, but my flesh kicked in and I kept going. I chose to do it, and I was exposed to nudity—pornography. It was only for a few moments, and thankfully that's where it stopped, but still I had returned to my sin like a dog to its vomit (Prov. 26:11). *What? No!* How could I have done that after years of freedom? I wanted to beat myself up. I felt like a fraud; I felt defeated. I knew Christ had died for this sin, and God forgave me, but I felt like a hypocrite. I know many of you are all too familiar with this cycle, whether in that particular sin struggle or another.

To make things worse, a few days later I was slated to preach a message in front of a few thousand young adults on Romans 8:5–13, about choosing to let God instead of our flesh be in the driver's seat of our lives. How could I teach and preach God's Word and tell them to remove their flesh from the driver's seat when my own flesh so recently had its foot mashed on the gas pedal? I knew I had a choice—to stay silent about my sin or to expose it. To live out either Psalm 32:3 or Proverbs 28:13. So I got behind the pulpit, and I . . .

What would you do, if you were in that moment? Be honest. What's your first reaction? These are questions and decisions you must deal with.

I began the message and made most of my points, but then I paused.[1] I walked the audience through the specifics of what I just told you, laying out exactly how it started, what I did, and how it ended. I told them I wanted them to know I struggle and sin too, and I wasn't onstage hypocritically calling them to deal with their flesh in a way I myself was unwilling to. I confessed my sin to them and asked for their forgiveness.

What do you think happened? Do you think they bolted for the exits, eager to get as far away as they could from yet another pastor with a moral failure?

After every message I gave at The Porch, I would stay down by the stage to talk and pray with anyone who wanted to. There was also a whole team of volunteers who did the same thing as pastors to their peers. After this message, I had the longest line I've ever had of people waiting to talk with me. There was a clear pattern. One after another, they told me, "I've never heard a pastor say that." "I've never had a pastor say anything like that." Then they poured out their struggles, told me where they were and how they were doing, and asked me how to find freedom from their sin. In that moment, it felt like the purest form of ministry that anyone could experience. God took my mess and used it as a message to point people back to freedom and forgiveness in Christ.

How Transparent Is Your Church?

Wherever I serve and lead in ministry, our team is committed to being transparent. Being "authentic in our walk" is one of The Porch's stated core values.[2] It wasn't just stated, though—it was (and is) lived. We don't just admit to being sinners; we also confess our specific sins and talked about our struggles with whoever needed to know them. The level of transparency I described above may be shocking to you, but its purpose isn't shock value. It's about refusing to let anyone put us on a pedestal as we pursue Christ together. It's about being sober-minded in our judgment of ourselves, not thinking of ourselves "more highly than [we] ought" (Rom. 12:3). We are just like those who hear our messages—sinners saved by grace who are continually in desperate need for the freeing truth of the gospel. This is part of the culture and DNA of Watermark, from those who teach from the stage to those who lead the janitorial team.

Is the leadership in your church vulnerable, authentic, and transparent? Are you? If not, that's a major reason why you won't be able to reach young adults.

Think about it. If a pastor or church staffer just admits to being a sinner in general, what kinds of sins do you automatically think they're referring to? Probably the kinds of sins people might feel comfortable admitting to in church, like not reading the Bible enough, not giving enough money, or possibly not sharing the gospel as often as they should. Or, God forbid, maybe they got just slightly frustrated when that person cut them off in traffic and thought a bad word but didn't say it out loud. How relatable is that, when young adults are struggling with much deeper and darker issues and sins like crippling anxiety, addictions of all kinds, abortions, and highly promiscuous relationships? Not very. If those "churchy" sins are true, then they need to be confessed. But what's also probably true is those church leaders need to confess their lustful thoughts about another person's spouse, the conflict they had with their own spouse, and the covetous materialism they're fighting when they look at the kinds of cars their church members drive but they can't afford to. Now we're talking. Now we're connecting and engaging.

Young adults know their leaders aren't perfect. They know they sin in way more areas than just not reading their Bibles enough. They know you're not perfect. But if you never talk about your own sins, or if all you admit to are those "churchy" sins or to just being a sinner like it's an abstract concept you deal with on your own, your lack of authenticity will drive them away because it doesn't show them how to address the sins they're really struggling with.

How Transparent Is Your Future Church?

I say this so passionately because shortly after I made that confession from the stage at The Porch, I was speaking at a seminary about the topic of reaching young adults. I told the exact same story to them. After I spoke, the students filled out feedback forms about the session. As I read through the feedback, I was heartbroken at how many future pastors and teachers said things like, "You just can't talk like that in a mixed-gender audience." "You can't say those words in front of people." "That's offensive." "You need to have the appearance of holiness as you preach to people." "You don't need to let them into your personal sins." "You can confess those in private."

This made me really sad. If you agree with their feedback, I'd discourage you from ministering to young adults (or anyone, really) until you can see authenticity is actually an advantage in ministry. The world does not need any more inauthentic pastors. If you want young adults to think you are the expert and you have it all together, you are unqualified for the job. If, however, you are willing to let them know how you struggle, when you struggle, and that you are quite literally a mess—that's the first step. Jesus takes your mess and makes it a message, or even a ministry. If you are unwilling to do that—and I say this as humbly and respectfully as I possibly can—you will not reach young adults. You just won't. You will take your mentality to the grave, looking back at a demographic you missed because you were not willing to be honest, real, transparent, and authentic.

CHAPTER 2

Teach the Whole Truth

A couple years ago, my single and twentysomething friend Amber was living it up in a Florida high-rise and working a corporate marketing job. She had just become a Christian and wanted to follow Jesus wholeheartedly, but didn't really know what that meant or how to do it. She'd been living with her boyfriend but they had just broken up, and she was struggling with her view on dating and how it fit into her new convictions and beliefs.

One of her best friends from high school, a girl she used to party with who had also recently trusted Christ, was living in Hawaii at the time and texted her a screenshot picture with a message saying, "You have to listen to this." "This" was a Porch podcast message called "Dating Decisions."[1] Amber listened to it all the way through, and then she played it again twice more the same day. She later told me one of the things that jumped out to her was a line about purity in dating that said something like, "How do you know if you've gone too far physically? When your body starts preparing itself for sex." She told me she'd never heard a pastor say something so explicit, clear, practical, and applicable. The realness drew her in.

When she looked up The Porch online, she saw we were a young adult ministry in Dallas. Since she didn't live close by, she just started devouring the podcasts, eventually listening to all our messages. As she did, she became increasingly convinced that following Christ should affect *all* areas of her life, especially dating. Being a Christian wasn't just something she was supposed to do on Sundays. This concept was new to her, but as the messages took biblical principles and made them applicable to her life, she developed in her faith. She got plugged into a local church in Florida and grew a ton.

I first heard about Amber's story when she showed up at The Porch in person one Tuesday night, having tagged along on her sister's business trip to Dallas so she could check it out for herself. There's a lot more to her journey after that moment, including eventually moving to Dallas, joining the church staff, and meeting her husband there, but that's another story. It all started when she heard God's timeless truth delivered in a way that resonated with her life as a young adult living in today's world.

Once you have a foundation of authenticity, you should use it to teach the entire counsel of God in a way that applies to real life. If you want to reach young adults, you have to show them how the entire Bible applies to their lives and help it make sense to them in the twenty-first century.

Theology, the Gospel, and Snapchat

The church has a lot of work to do to equip the next generation to understand and apply the full counsel of God. This isn't just about a lack of basic theological knowledge—though this is a big problem with this generation too—it's about the struggle to translate the wisdom principles in Scripture to their modern lives. What does Scripture say about dating? It's not exactly addressed, since dating is a recent concept in the grand scheme of things. What about online dating? Snapchat? Social media in general?

Let's go back to basic theology for a minute. A recent survey found most professing Christians hold some form of heretical views.[2] A few "highlights" from this study include:

- 60 percent believe everyone eventually goes to heaven.
- More than half believe Jesus was the first and greatest being created by God.
- 64 percent believe God accepts the worship of all religions.
- 74 percent believe small sins don't warrant eternal damnation.
- 44 percent believe the Bible contains helpful myths but isn't literally true.
- 77 percent believe people must contribute their own effort for personal salvation.

Not every person who took the survey was a Christian, but the majority of respondents claimed to be. That last one especially breaks my heart. The "gospel of good works" pervades the cultural Christianity of so many young adults, where they believe they must somehow earn their way to heaven. I've had conversations with thousands of young adults over the years, and there are two questions I ask just about everyone. The first one is, "On a scale of 1 to 10, with 10 being absolutely certain and 1 being not so sure, how certain are you that if you died today, you'd go to heaven to be with God?" After they respond, my follow-up question is, "If you were to stand before God and he asked why he should let you into heaven, what would you say?"

The answer to the first question is often something less than "10," because they don't have assurance of salvation. This is sad but doesn't surprise me, since only 50 percent of younger Millennials believe in God and are absolutely certain about it.[3] And even when they do say "10," their response to the second question frequently includes some version of, "Well, I've been a pretty good person . . . I try to love God . . . I help other people." This is an outworking of the moralistic therapeutic deism that's been eroding orthodox Christianity in our country, where people believe God basically wants them to be good and nice, and good people go to heaven.[4] They're sincere—but they're sincerely wrong and damned for it. This may sound harsh, but it isn't my idea—it's God's (Gal. 2:16). Simply put, that is not what the Bible teaches about how to be saved. And I'm afraid that just like the pictures and videos on Snapchat disappear a few seconds after you view them, a right understanding of theology and the gospel has all but disappeared in young adults too.

How about the Bible?

The Bible is the most widely read book on earth—more than five billion copies have been sold.[5] For a long time, nearly half of Americans reported reading the Bible once a week or more, but that number continues to decline. This might not be surprising, given that fewer than 25 percent of Americans believe the Bible is the literal Word of God, which is the lowest percentage Gallup has recorded in forty years.[6] The Bible is showing up on modern lists of books you don't have to bother reading.[7] Now, fewer than 25 percent of Millennials claim to read the Bible at least once a week or more. Nearly half of Millennials are neutral or skeptical toward the Bible.[8] They're twice as likely as their elders to say the Bible is just another book of teachings written by humans.[9] When you're teaching the Bible to young adults, you're fighting an uphill battle against biblical illiteracy and skepticism. But it's a battle that can be won.

Whenever I teach young adults, I see more smartphones than physical Bibles when the crowd looks up a text (a biblical text . . . though they get plenty of the other kind too). The rise of Bible apps has made the Scriptures more accessible to millions of people. The YouVersion Bible app has been downloaded more than three hundred million times, by people in every country on earth.[10] This is incredible! It also comes with some challenges. By reading the Bible with an app and jumping from verse to verse, a sense of the entirety of Scripture can be missed. People can look up the passages mentioned in the sermon with no sense of context, overall narrative, or what came before or after. It's also easier to proof-text verses in support of unorthodox views, or pick and choose pieces of doctrine to highlight only the ones appealing to modern cultural sensibilities. Though access to the Scriptures is at the highest point ever, biblical illiteracy may also be at crisis levels.[11]

Remedial Education

I include all these statistics and observations not to discourage you but to give you a sense of the monumental challenge facing the church in engaging the next generation with the Scriptures. If we really believe we're speaking "the very words of God" (1 Pet. 4:11) and all Scripture is inspired by God and is useful for "teaching, rebuking, correcting and training" young adults (2 Tim. 3:16), how do we get them to understand the Bible and apply it to their lives?

Part of the answer comes from the secular marketplace, because this lack of knowledge in today's young adults isn't limited to the Scriptures. Companies like Home Depot, Procter & Gamble, and Sherwin-Williams are hosting classes and online tutorials for young adults on things like how to mow a lawn, use a tape measure, hammer a nail, and pick a paint color.[12] Many Millennials don't know how to do things like this—they largely grew up with overscheduled childhoods, tech-dependent lifestyles, and delayed adulthood. They need remedial education before they can make an informed purchasing decision or take on a project in certain areas. I'm obviously painting with a broad brush here, and no doubt there are many exceptions to this, but it's a big enough trend that multiple Fortune 500 companies are looking to capitalize on it.

Here's the application: if you want to reach young adults, especially those who are unchurched, you'll need to start with the basics. As you share the gospel, make apologetic arguments, and unpack the Scriptures, you need to pay special attention to explaining what things mean. We're talking *basic*. Stay away from "Christianese" that wouldn't make sense to someone who didn't grow up in church or go to seminary. Don't assume they'll understand something when you say it the first time. When I'm preparing messages for Millennials, I'm always thinking about how to break down the truth into bite-sized pieces someone with no background in the church could understand. You need to do this with everything, from unpacking theological concepts to explaining who the Bible characters are. Many young adults didn't grow up with felt-board Sunday school stories, so they might not know who Moses and David are, let alone what *justification* and *propitiation* mean. Explain, explain, explain. That's what it means to teach—you explain.

What Should You Be Teaching?

All of the Bible. Next question?

Well, let me unpack this a bit. I mean you should literally teach all of God's Word, not shying away from any of the hard stuff that takes some wrestling to get through. Is God a moral monster for what he commanded the Israelites to do when they settled in the promised land? Lean into it. Is premarital sex a sin? Be clear. Is online dating unwise? Explain what principles apply. Are homosexuality and transgenderism wrong? Make a clear case for a biblical sexual ethic. Be firm where the Bible is firm and flexible where the Bible is flexible.

If anything, I have a bias toward leaning into and running toward the tough topics that don't easily fit in with the modern current of culture. I am willing to talk openly about sex, pornography, masturbation, dating, transgenderism, homosexuality, anxiety, depression, suicide, singleness, marriage, divorce, remarriage, money, work, evangelism, and much more, all from a biblical point of view. The topic you are nervous to cover is most likely exactly what you should teach next.

This takes some courage, but don't we believe the teachings of Scripture are not old-fashioned ideas with no bearing on life today but rather the way God has fashioned life to work best? We should want to teach the entirety of Scripture, unpacking what it says and how it applies to the lives of modern young adults. If people are having conversations in culture, we should want to equip them with a biblical worldview of why God's way works.

Apply the Truth to Life Today

As I teach the whole truth of God, I try to help my audience understand and apply what God's Word says to their cultural realities. I hope to show them how the Bible should make a difference in their lives. Millennial Christians need guidance on how to engage culture in a meaningful way, and to do so from a distinctly Christian perspective. They want this from their leaders—one of the most powerful motivations for Christian Millennials to practice their faith is to find ways to bring the teachings of Jesus to the problems and issues they encounter in their lives and the world.[13] Show them how the Bible should impact their personal purity, their relationships and friendships, their work, their money, their goals for life . . . everything. Even if you're preaching to people who don't believe the Bible is the inspired Word of God—and I do hope some people who don't know Christ are also attending your gatherings—you should be making a case for how God's Word and God's way best represent the ideal way to live, even apart from theology. We're just talking about wisdom here, the way life works.

Take discontentment, for example. Sure, the Bible tells us we should be content with what we have (1 Tim. 6:6–7), but did you know complaining has also been found to shrink the hippocampus, an area of the brain that's critical to problem solving and intelligent thought?[14] What person wants to shrink their brain?

Or how about money? The thousands-of-years-old Bible says to watch out for greed (Luke 12:15), and modern research shows making more money beyond a certain level is associated with reduced life satisfaction and a lower level of well-being,[15] and being generous boosts the brain's health.[16]

Or let's talk about lust and marriage. Sure, the Bible says to avoid lust because it's an adulterous sin (Matt. 5:28), but research has also discovered that married people who quickly disengage their attention from an attractive person are less likely to engage in infidelity, and their marriages are more likely to last.[17] What about living together before marriage? The Bible says to save the marriage bed (sex) for marriage (Heb. 13:4). Some people claim the "cohabitation effect" no longer raises the chance of a couple getting divorced as the practice becomes more normal in today's young adults, but recent research confirms premarital cohabitation still increases the likelihood of divorce.[18]

Or let's talk forgiveness for a second. The Bible says to forgive generously (Eph. 4:32), but this isn't just a healthy spiritual practice—science shows whether or not you're a forgiving person can significantly affect your physical health.[19]

I could go on and on—there are so many examples of how God's Word is demonstrably true from what we observe in the world around us and in our own brains and bodies. The Bible applies to life, no matter what you believe. Show people this, and they'll be more likely to listen.

When the Bible Isn't Clear

In many areas, the Bible provides clear instruction on what we should and shouldn't do. But there are also some things that aren't quite as clear, and young adults need help in applying the Bible to the decisions they're facing. Let's take alcohol as a classic example. It's still a relevant topic, even though other issues have replaced it in the spotlight of many church conversations. Nearly three-quarters of all adults in the US drink alcohol,[20] and trends in today's young adults range from being "sober curious"[21] to getting "päntsdrunk."[22] What should you be telling them?

It's 100 percent clear in Scripture we shouldn't get drunk (Eph. 5:18), but it's also clear we have the freedom to drink moderately (1 Tim. 5:23)—except some people struggle with alcoholism and can't safely drink at all. Since the answer to "Can I have this drink?" depends on the situation and the people involved, you could possibly call it a gray area. The Bible does give us guidelines for how to handle such gray areas, and I keep a list of questions written down that I use to clarify whether something is a good idea or not.

These "Don't do it if . . ." questions apply when considering whether the Bible would advise against something:

- "Will it have negative long-term consequences?" Two things immediately come to mind here. One is unwise and unaffordable debt, which can put you in financial bondage. The other is addiction, which is why some people are OK having a single drink while other people have to abstain (1 Cor. 6:12).

- "Could it harm my body, God's temple?" Anything that's likely to bring bad health or disease should be avoided. Often this comes down to moderation: a cigar every once in a while might not be a problem, but cigars every day could lead to cancer or other ailments. For other things, like shooting up drugs, even once would be defiling (Rom. 6:13; 1 Cor. 6:19–20).

- "Will it give me a guilty conscience?" Basically, if you think something is wrong, don't do it. For example, I know some people think it is a sin to drink any alcohol at all, even though the Bible doesn't say that. If you take a drink while thinking it's wrong, it means you're choosing to do what you think God has forbidden. You're choosing to disobey, and that's wrong (Rom. 14:23; 1 Cor. 8:7).

- "Will it cause someone else to sin?" This is where we can lovingly sacrifice a little bit of our freedom to help our brothers and sisters. An example would be a friend who I know is a recovering alcoholic: I would choose not to drink when around them so there's no temptation for them to join in (Rom. 13:10; 1 Cor. 8:9–13).

- "Will it hurt my witness?" We don't want to hinder the spread of the gospel, and you never know who may be watching. As a believer, your life should stand out as different—but in a good way (1 Cor. 10:32–33; 1 Pet. 3:15–17).

If the answer to all five of those questions is no, then it seems the action won't cause any harm. It's not clearly a bad idea. But is it a good idea? I have a couple more questions I use to help figure that out. For these, you're looking for a yes.

- "Will it benefit either myself or others?" Some things may not have a negative impact, but may not be positive either. Preferably, you'd want to spend your time doing something beneficial (1 Cor. 10:23–24).

- "Will it bring glory to God?" Whatever you do, your goal should be to glorify God, not to glorify yourself (1 Cor. 10:31).

Teaching the next generation how to apply the Bible to the gray areas of their lives will make it useful to them on an everyday basis.

How We Do It

The messages I have given at The Porch aren't the best teaching ever heard, I can promise you. I honestly believe more life change has come out of the conversations I have seen people have with Porch volunteers after the message than from what people heard during the message. But teaching does matter. I consistently heard from listeners that the messages explained and applied the Bible in a way that resonated freshly with them. I'll let you know the principles informing how I prepared my messages and series in a bit, but I'd also like to give you a chance to hear some of them for yourself, if you'd like to get a sense of exactly how this is done.[23] Here are some message series around the main topics consistently covered at The Porch:

- **Anxiety:** the "Exhale" series
- **Love, Sex, Dating, and Marriage:** the "First Comes Love" series, the "Relationship Goals" series, the "Unrestricted" series
- **Living as a Christian:** the "Bad Advice" series, the "Vice & Virtue" series
- **Growing Up:** the "Adulting" series
- **The Life and Teachings of Jesus:** the "AD" series
- **Understanding the Old Testament:** the "BC" series[24]

The Porch blog also teaches truth in written form.[25] You can read posts with titles such as:

- "10 Ways to Ruin Your Life in Your 20s" (the most-read post)

- "How to Know if You've Found the One"
- "10 Things a Woman Should Look for in a Man"
- "Why Premarital Sex Is a Bad Idea"
- "10 Things a Man Should Look for in a Woman"
- "How to Overcome a Pornography Addiction"
- "10 Things to Do While You're Single"

I'm not saying these are the best posts you'll ever read on the topics, but they'll give you an idea of ways to engage young adults with the truth of God's Word.

Having a Plan

At The Porch I taught a blend of series based on specific topics and walk-throughs of books of the Bible. I would typically alternate topical series and book-based series, but that wasn't a rule. At the beginning of each year, our teaching team went on a "teaching retreat" where we would talk through the topics we'd like to cover for the year and get a general sense of how many weeks we planned to spend on each topic. We tried to cover some topics every year, like dating, sex, anxiety/worry, work, purpose, community, money, and evangelism. This was partly because we had a lot of new people attending The Porch throughout the year who hadn't heard previous messages on these topics, and partly because pretty much all young adults could use continual reminding and encouragement in these areas, which are "top of mind" for many of them.

We also tried to be responsive to what was happening in culture as we planned out our messages, knowing we'd need to shepherd and equip people based on current events, so we always built some flexibility into the plan. Another big objective of getting away was for our teaching team to deepen in trust, grow relationally, and protect our friendships from any kind of competitive spirit.

This method isn't a prescription, but if you have regular teaching responsibilities, I'd encourage you to come up with a way that works for you to think strategically about the truth you want to communicate over the course of the next few months or a year. Don't just wing it from week to week.

Preparing a Message

It's hard to put together a reasonably decent message every week, let alone a great one. I found it extremely helpful to have a standard process for creating my messages. I'll give it to you— it's not a perfect method, but these eight principles worked well for me and my team, and you can adapt them to your context.

- **Start with a team.** Porch messages are team projects from start to finish. I never wrote a message completely by myself. We had at least three people and as many as ten involved. The team was incredibly helpful in analyzing the biblical text and coming up with illustration ideas. Have you ever started a pull-start lawn mower? You yank the string, and it makes a sound for a moment. You do that again, and again, until the engine starts to run. This is what we were doing. We'd pull the string of creativity and debate what the Scriptures said, and the momentum started to build the message. It was mostly just discussions about the Bible.

- **Outsource your weaknesses.** Even the most creative leaders and teachers thrive on teams, but let's say you struggle to come up with creative illustrations. Find the most creative people you have access to, and invite them to influence your sermon early in the process. Some may be staff people, and others may be volunteers. Remember the movie *Ocean's 11*? They built a team of expert role players with different areas of expertise to pull off robbing a casino. Similarly, build a team of experts to help pull off writing an amazing sermon.

- **Follow an outline.** Find a template that works for you. You do not need a perfect method; you need a consistent method. Resist the urge to "reinvent the wheel" week to week. There are a lot of outlines out there. I have a strong bias toward mine (see below), and I think it's transferable. It is made up of the best things I've heard from others over the years. When you go on a road trip, you have a plan. When you go to write a message, start with a path to follow, otherwise known as an outline.

- **Know your audience.** Be a student of your listeners. Stay relevant. Take note of current events, recent news, and popular culture. Beware of assumptions, though—your flock may or may not reflect the trends of their generation. I've heard from one particular Christian recording artist that he writes songs for

"Becky." Becky is a fictitious, generalized character who listens to Christian radio. Whenever I wrote a message for The Porch, I wrote it for "Johnny and Jane Dallas." They are single, interested in faith, stuck in the world, distracted by concerns for the future, very busy, and bored with life.

- **Practice.** Don't just talk through your sermon points beforehand; give the message in advance like you're really teaching it. Preparation does not push out the Holy Spirit's influence, but disorganization and pro-crastination might. Said otherwise, I've found the Holy Spirit has an affinity for using preparedness. So, get ready to be excellent by practicing what you preach . . . literally.

- **Teach the Bible . . . all of it.** We are communicating truth that is not our own. We should bring our best energy *to* the text and get our best energy *from* the text. Don't leave any part of it out.

- **Be you.** Preaching is the Bible poured through person-ality. Authenticity and brutal honesty are a win. People want to follow real people. Present yourself as you are, not as you'd like to be seen. Be vulnerable. Be you.

- **Get feedback.** You need truth tellers and people who will "faithfully wound" you if something wasn't excel-lent. There is no perfect sermon; give others the free-dom to talk about the imperfections so you can grow from it. Every leadership opportunity you have is an op-portunity to improve as a leader. But remember, not all feedback is created equal.

Have an Outline

It's helpful to not feel like you're starting from scratch when you put together the structure of your message. I consistently followed a standard outline for our messages. Having this structure actually helped our creativity rather than hindered it, since it allowed our creativity to be focused on the content of the message rather than the framework of it. Here's what I used, in this exact order:

- **Image:** A captivating image or illustration that sets the subject up well and can be referenced throughout the message.
- **Need:** Why this message is so important. Answers the audience's question of, "Why should I listen for the next twenty-five minutes?"
- **Subject:** What we will be talking about.
- **Preview:** Tell them what we are going to tell them, giving a preview of the three points or whatever we are going to say about the subject.
- **Text Address:** Where in the Scriptures we will be.
- **Setup:** Context, characters, geography, author, time, and so on.
- **Text:** Read the text or the first section of the text.
- **Point #1** that supports the subject and is pulled from the text.
  - Explaining what point #1 means
    - Supporting idea and Scripture
    - Supporting idea and Scripture
    - Supporting idea and Scripture

- Explaining why point #1 is important
  - Supporting idea and Scripture
  - Supporting idea and Scripture
  - Supporting idea and Scripture
- Explaining what we should do about point #1
  - Supporting idea and Scripture
  - Illustration about point #1 or your subject, incorporating your explanations
  - Transition connecting point #1 to point #2, and/or back to the text
- **Point #2 and #3**—same outline as for point #1
- **Summary:** Tell them what you told them, giving a recap of your three points (consider repeating your preview).
- **Closing:** A closing image illustrating the subject and supporting ideas with the application.

Having three points made the message easy to follow. Explaining what the points meant, why they mattered, and what to do about them allowed me to set up my applications in a way that made sense to the young adults in the audience. Find a good outline and stick with it, and you'll find your messages become easier to create and understand.

Wielding the Sword

Having an outline is great, but don't let an outline—or any of the other thoughts I've shared in this chapter—reach canonical status in your teaching. Sometimes we just need to get out of the way and let the truth speak for itself! God's Word is living and active, sharper than any sword (Heb. 4:12). It can fight for itself. That said, while you can't dull this blade, you can definitely wield it poorly. I hope these ideas are helpful as you work hard to be someone who "correctly handles the [s]word of truth" (2 Tim. 2:15).

CHAPTER 3

Get Good Feedback

It's Tuesday at 5:30 p.m., and The Porch is going to start in just an hour and a half. That means nearly four thousand young adults are going to flood the auditorium I'm currently sitting in. They'll want to hear a compelling message from the Bible that they can apply to their lives. I thought I had one to give them, but now I just feel like I've been punched in the gut by a UFC fighter.

Here's the problem: I just gave the message I had prepared to a panel of trusted critics, and they told me it needed a lot of work. A lot of work? In an hour! I still need to meet with the tech team and worship band to review and pray for the evening's service. This means I have just an hour to fix a message that they said was "confusing," "lacked cohesiveness," "needed more illustrations," "needed new points," and "needed a new main idea." That's practically a total rewrite—in an hour.

I've become pretty accustomed to it, because I believe feedback makes my messages better. I'm also grateful I won't be giving the subpar message I had originally prepared to thousands of people. Moreover, the message I give will be a team effort, built by a team of trusted theologians. So I get to work.

Every Message Gets a Grade

Before I ever gave a message at The Porch, I'd already preached it to a team of critics who gave it a number grade (0–100), provided specific critiques, and brainstormed suggestions on how to make it better. Sometimes I only needed to make a few changes; other times I needed to make significant changes, and on some occasions it was a total rewrite. Every time, the message I ended up preaching was better because of the wisdom contained in the counsel I'd received (Prov. 15:22).

It didn't stop there. By ten o'clock the next morning, every person on our Porch staff team would send me an email with a number grade on how the evening and message had gone, along with at least one thing that went well and at least one thing that could be improved. I would read every word and digest the takeaways on how we could continue to make things even more excellent.

But I'm not the only one who would get a grade—just about anyone teaching at The Porch would get one too. This exercise helped our team think like owners, and it helped the communicators and worship leaders improve.

You might say I'm a fanatic about feedback. I'd probably add it to my list of personal "love languages." Yes, you read that correctly. Feedback is my love language. I love getting it, I love giving it, and I love to help others love it too. I've heard it said, "Great leaders eat feedback for breakfast." Feedback just might be the most important meal of my day.

Would Jesus Give Feedback?

"Wait, you get a *grade* for every message? That's not the gospel!" I've been told something like that plenty of times. But in fact, the gospel allows me to sleep well at night, no matter what my grade was. The gospel frees me from finding identity in a grade. It isn't just that my mistakes and sins are forgiven, allowing me to preach on another Tuesday evening; it's the power of God at work (Rom. 1:16). The Lord Almighty can do anything with the scraps I lay before him and others with my preaching, whether my message was a 50 or a 99. I rest easy, knowing God is in control.

Are we following Jesus's example? Did he tell people hard truths to help them grow? I sure think so. Here's an example: a crowd of people was waiting for Jesus to come down from the mountain where he was transfigured. One of the people waiting was a man with a demon-possessed son. He had begged the disciples to cast it out, and they tried but couldn't. So the man waited for Jesus and fell at his feet once he rejoined the crowd, begging Jesus to heal his boy. Before Jesus did anything else, he said to the people, "O faithless and twisted generation, how long am I to be with you? How long am I to bear with you?" (Matt. 17:17 ESV).

Whoa! Faithless? Twisted? That's some pretty harsh feedback, Jesus. You can almost imagine him rubbing his forehead like an exasperated parent. "Haven't we covered this already?" Jesus didn't mince words or hesitate in calling out the disciples and crowd for not having the necessary faith to heal the boy.

After Jesus healed the child, his disciples asked him privately why they couldn't cast out the demon. He told them, "Because of your little faith. For truly, I say to you, if you have faith like a grain of mustard seed, you will say to this mountain, 'Move from here to there,' and it will move, and nothing will be impossible for you" (v. 20 ESV).

He told them what was wrong, and he coached them on what they needed to do instead. At the right time, in the right place, Jesus delivered direct yet loving feedback.

Beyond Jesus's specific example here, I believe Scripture as a whole supports this idea. After all, isn't all Scripture useful for "teaching, rebuking, correcting and training" (2 Tim. 3:16–17)? That sounds a lot like feedback to me.

A Make-Out Session

Why do we go through all this? Well, who doesn't enjoy a nice kiss? Scripture says the honest answers we give one another are like a "kiss on the lips" (Prov. 24:26). A few years ago, another very gifted Watermark staff guy gave a message at The Porch. He wasn't in our regular teaching rotation, so it was a new experience for him. The next morning, he sat down with the team to go through everyone's feedback just like I always did. We had a lot to say, and it wasn't all congratulatory. In fact, most of it was constructive.

This young man excelled at everything he did. He's the guy who made straight As and did well in sports. He was not used to hearing he hadn't aced it. It wasn't at all easy or fun for him to hear, but as he was leaving the room, he looked back at us and said with a wink, "Thanks for the make-out session!" He didn't like it, but he understood the feedback was a gift given in love, and hating the correction would have been stupid (Prov. 12:1). Yes, the Bible literally calls you stupid if you hate correction. Don't be stupid.

I get and give feedback because it helps me excel. I believe excellence honors God and inspires people, so I try to make everything we do more excellent. I get feedback because I want to remove any possible stumbling block that might keep someone from hearing and responding to the truth of God's Word (2 Cor. 6:3). I also do this because I want to be as effective and relevant as possible, doing whatever it takes to get the gospel message in front of as many people as possible, in a way they can understand and relate to (1 Cor. 9:22).

Feedback Has a Double Benefit

I also focus on feedback because it doesn't just develop the person getting the feedback; it also develops the person *giving it*. Here are a few lines from an email I would send every time a new person joined our Porch staff team, letting them know about the feedback process:

> This serves several purposes, but PRIMARILY this exercise is for YOU. It teaches you to think critically. To always have an opinion. To learn how to improve on communication. To capture best practices on production. Let me say it again, because you might not have believed me—this exercise has more to do with your development than anything else. . . . Consider this: most often in life, the value you will bring to something (a team, a position, an event, etc.) will be determined solely by your ability to make it better. If you can't make it better, or if it would be better without your contribution, then you were not a "value-add." If, however, you can assess what needs improvement and what is going well, then you are already halfway to adding value to anything you are a part of. It's important.

It will make you better. People who excel are people who are always thinking about how to make something more excellent.

This feedback wasn't just limited to Porch messages, and Porch staff members weren't the only ones whom I asked for feedback from or gave feedback to. Volunteers and leaders got and gave feedback too. After just about every significant event or activity, we asked questions like these:

- What can we celebrate and thank God for?
- What worked well?
- What could have been better?
- What challenges did we face?
- Were there any consistent themes in participant feedback?
- How well did we steward our resources?
- Would we do it again?

As we thought through the answers to those questions, our team built an "OFI list" so we didn't forget what we learned— the various "Opportunities For Improvement" we had received. When we would go to do the event again, or something similar, we could refer back to these lists to help us make things even more excellent.

An Important Distinction

There's an important nuance about feedback I want to tell you about before we go further. Thinking critically is a valuable skill.

It helps people notice things, question things, connect things, and make things better. You want every leader at every level to be thinking about how to make things better. But if *thinking critically* is a skill, *being critical* is equally a snare. The line between these two things can be razor-thin, but the differences between them are vast. One will grow your team, and the other will tear it down. Watch out for cynicism, and don't just focus on the problems—spend your best energy on solutions. Don't just tear things down; be sure to build them up as well.

How to Get Good Feedback

If you want to develop yourself and your team, you should make it a point to give and receive feedback regularly. But if you don't naturally love feedback, you need to learn to love it, and you need to intentionally create feedback channels for whatever your ministry context is. Repetition helps. This will take time, effort, and intentionality, but I believe it will result in much fruit. As a leader, you must *invite* feedback, *celebrate* feedback, and *respond* to feedback.

Inviting Feedback

Unless you tell them you want it, most people won't give you the feedback you need. You need to ask them, very specifically, to give you feedback. Give people the authority and freedom to say what they are really thinking and to be brutally honest with you (and be sure not to bite their head off if they do). Create a space and a method to request and deliver feedback. Let people know before the event or message that you will be asking for feedback afterward. You may need to ask a specific list of questions to get the feedback process started, since sometimes it can be hard to know where to start if you keep things too general.

Now, I've worked with a preacher who wore himself out trying to take and apply everyone's feedback. The problem is not everyone's feedback is worth applying. I had to coach him on how to know what to apply and what to just listen to and acknowledge. When you do start to regularly get feedback, you'll quickly understand not all feedback is created equal. You should invite it from everyone involved (remember, it's also part of their development), but you'll likely find there's a consistent group of people who give you the most valuable feedback. Remember, you can't invite feedback just from your fans ("That message was incredible . . . just like every other one you've preached!") or your foes ("That was terrible . . . why are you even in ministry?").

Whatever you do, don't overlook feedback from some of the most valuable people in your ministry: the new folks. Every year we added a few new people to the circle, and every year I sent the same email reminding them how valuable their "fresh eyes" were. When people have fresh eyes and don't share all of your assumptions and experiences, they can provide some of the best feedback you'll ever get. Never waste the first few months of a new team member's time in your ministry by not giving them a voice into the feedback loop, because before you know it, they will "go native" and lose their fresh perspective.

Celebrating Feedback

One of the most effective ways to get great feedback is to celebrate it. Put a spotlight on the person and the feedback you found so valuable. What gets recognized and rewarded gets repeated. Be sure to not just celebrate positive feedback. Shine a bright light on the truths that were hard but helpful for you to hear. Let your entire team know who gave you constructive feedback, how grateful you are for it, how much you value that kind of input from everyone, and what you plan to do with it.

Responding to Feedback

This kind of high-feedback culture only works well in an environment of humility and trust. People must be able to trust that you will receive any feedback they give with an attitude of humility and gratitude. Like I mentioned before, you can't bite someone's head off when they give you input that's hard to receive and then expect them to keep courageously giving it to you. Getting defensive or combative will severely limit the quality and quantity of the feedback you get.

And, perhaps most importantly, *do* something with the feedback you get. If you never truly prove you're listening to the feedback by making changes and doing things differently, soon you'll be surrounded by people who have nothing significant to say. A "yes man" might pad your ego, but he or she won't help you grow.

Giving Great Feedback

Your team will grow when they learn to give great feedback to you and others, but they'll also grow when you give great feedback to them. I've led teams of young adults for more than a decade, and I've learned the way they expect, receive, and process feedback is significantly different from the generations before them. These principles of feedback-giving can be applied to employees and volunteers alike.

- **Initiate the conversation.** As a leader, it's your responsibility to provide great feedback to the people who are working with you. Your good intentions of providing helpful feedback won't cut it; you must carve out the time to have feedback conversations. This might be a challenge for you, as 69 percent of managers report they are uncomfortable with communicating to their employees in general, and 37 percent are especially uncomfortable with giving feedback.[1] Millennials have been inundated with feedback their whole lives, from parents, teachers, coaches, and so on. They're surprised when they don't get great feedback in the workplace. If they get regular feedback, they'll be better employees—engagement nearly doubles when a supervisor provides feedback at least monthly.[2]

- **Give feedback consistently throughout the year.** An annual or even semiannual review doesn't cut it. You can't hoard all of your thoughts, comments, and documents about a person's performance throughout the year only to pounce on them during review season with 365 days' worth of "constructive criticism" and expect there to be positive results. Young adults are expecting feedback in real time, and they respond best to it when it's given right after the activity it applies to. The world at large gives them near-instant feedback (for example, how many "likes" an Instagram post gets in a couple hours), and they expect their work and service environments to do the same.

- **Give positive feedback.** Be sure to include a generous amount of positive feedback. A Gallup survey found that 67 percent of employees whose managers focused on their strengths were fully engaged in their work, as compared to only 31 percent of employees whose managers focused on their weaknesses.[3] According to the *Harvard Business Review*, high-performing teams give nearly six times more positive feedback than average teams.[4] Meanwhile, low-performing teams give nearly twice as much negative feedback as average teams. If you have a hard time sharing positive feedback, think about people's positive contributions you currently take for granted. Make a list, and let people know when you see their strengths in action. Building people's strengths is far more effective than fixating on their weaknesses.

- **Be specific.** For constructive feedback to be effective, it has to be concrete and actionable. Broad statements typically aren't helpful, but detailed ones are. You might feel bad about offering specific critiques, but remember you're doing it for their benefit and development. (Heart check: make sure you're doing it for that reason.) You can tell people things that are hard for them to hear as long as they know you love them and are for them. When providing feedback, set the context of what was happening, share your specific observation, explain the result of the behavior or performance you observed, and reaffirm (or establish for the first time) your expectations.

The Gift That Keeps on Giving

Feedback is a gift. When it's done well, it really can be a "love language" that takes you, your team, and your ministry to new levels. If you do not currently operate in a culture with lots of healthy feedback, I believe this is one of those shifts you can make that will provide near-instant positive results.

SECTION TWO

Engage

CHAPTER 4

Hold Traditions Loosely

A number of years ago, one of my friends was invited to interview for the role of senior pastor at an out-of-state church. He wasn't sure he would be a great fit with the church's style and culture, but he wanted to be faithful in considering the opportunity, so he made the trip. One of the first things my friend asked them when they sat down together was, "What are your church's sacred cows?" Their immediate response: "We don't have any." "Oh, really? What if we wanted to move the church service from Sundays to Saturdays?" "No, we couldn't do that—of course we'll keep meeting on Sundays like we always have." "OK, there's one sacred cow. Could we ever get rid of the organ?" "No way—that's an important part of our church's heritage, plus it would be expensive." "OK, that's two sacred cows. What if we stopped having Sunday school?" "Not a chance—we've always had Sunday school, and our people would definitely want to keep it." "Great," my friend said. "Those things are all fine, but can we just admit—you don't have a sacred cow; you've got the makings of a sacred herd!" Then they got to have a great conversation about methods to reach people in the most effective ways possible. He didn't end up taking the job, but he was able to challenge and sharpen their thinking about how they did ministry.

Is Change a Four-Letter Word to You?

How do you handle change? As with feedback, some people naturally love change and others hate it. I believe one of the main reasons the church has struggled to reach and engage young adults is it has a hard time dealing with change. Much like you must learn to love and embrace feedback to be an effective leader, you'll need to love and embrace healthy change if you want to reach this generation of young adults and the generations following them. Like I said earlier, if young adults are not joining and eventually leading in your church, it's going to die (and might already be dying).

One of the natural rhythms of any church is that, without intentional effort, it will grow old and irrelevant, eventually leaving itself one generational cycle away from shutting down. But it doesn't have to be this way. I believe it's possible for the church to vibrantly perpetuate itself by taking the never-changing message of the gospel to an ever-changing people. This can be done without compromising what we cannot compromise, and it isn't a new concept—the apostle Paul made it a priority to do exactly that in some of the first churches (1 Cor. 9:19–23).

We Get in Our Own Way

One big obstacle the church has in reaching the next generation is we have a hard time letting go of certain traditions. I'm
not saying all traditions are inherently bad. There's a reason
our hearts swell when we sing a timeless hymn, or when Mom
makes her classic meal at Thanksgiving or Christmas, or when
you revisit that certain place with your special someone. At its
best, church tradition is alive with meaning. Jaroslav Pelikan,
a Christian historian, said this: "Tradition is the living faith of
the dead, traditionalism is the dead faith of the living. And, I
suppose I should add, it is traditionalism that gives tradition
such a bad name."[1] It's a beautiful thing when traditions connect our hearts to shared memories and timeless truths. As the
modern church, we're following in the footsteps of those early
church founders who came before us. They're dead, but their
faith is still alive. We're reading the same Scriptures they read
thousands of years ago and worshiping the same God as a part
of the same body of Christ. That's powerful and meaningful.

But tradition has been made ultimate in many areas and has
trumped wisdom for many years when it comes to the church
reaching the next generation. Many traditions have become
dead rituals that are generally resistant to change. It might not
be a verbalized resistance, but it's there, one likely evidence
being the many thousands of churches in America that close
every year.[2] Some closures are surely for good reasons, but no
doubt more than a few are because the church failed to adapt
to reach people today in a way that would allow them to thrive.
This is a natural, destructive pattern if it's not intentionally
addressed. If a church is successful at reaching people in a

certain place and time, it's easy to get locked in to that way of thinking. There can be a sense of "We know what works, so we don't need to change it." The thing is, *culture is always changing*, so what worked before isn't going to keep working for long. Keeping certain traditions, practices, and styles when they've become silly or meaningless is counterproductive. On a macro scale, we can see one element of this playing out in how disinterested so many in the next generation are toward matters of faith. Hitting closer to home, young adults might not be connecting with your church because it feels awkward and out of touch. It might be so dissonant from the world and culture they live and breathe that they simply aren't interested in connecting with it. It's too foreign, too strange, and maybe even too "churchy."

Do words like *relevant*, *innovative*, and *adaptable* describe your church? If not, that's probably a reason why you're not reaching the next generation in the most effective way possible.

A Quick Heart Check

Talking about change can be scary and challenging. Before we go any further, I want to remind you of why this is such an important topic.

The greatest commandment Jesus gave his church is to love God and love others (Matt. 22:36–40). The Great Commission he gave his church is to make disciples of all people (28:19–20). When religious leaders in Jesus's day lost sight of those things, he gave them one of his harshest rebukes, telling them their worship was pointless and they had abandoned God's commands for the sake of following human traditions (Mark 7:6–9). Are you and your church doing the same?

Unexamined and unsurrendered traditions and practices can get in the way of your church loving God and loving people, and that's why you need to consider changing them. This isn't about being featured in *Christianity Today* or *Outreach* magazine, or hitting a particular growth rate, or being perceived as liturgical or contemporary. This isn't even about meeting the needs and desires of this particular generation of young adults, or any that follow—it's about overcoming any resistance you have to evaluating and changing whatever it is you're doing in order to increase your effectiveness for Christ, no matter who you're trying to reach. It's about developing the ability, discipline, and vision to evaluate what you're doing and make appropriate changes, whatever those changes are and whenever they need to be made, for the entire life of your church.

Maybe you're thinking, *I need my senior pastor to read this.* Hang on—we'll come back to that.

I'm not saying you have to change everything you're doing right now. How could I? I've probably never been to your church to see what you're doing and how it's working. For example, you might not be placed in a community where lots of young adults live, so it would be unreasonable to expect you'd attract droves of them. But I am telling you that you must be *willing* to change just about everything for the sake of the gospel. Doing this only means you're trying to get ready for what tomorrow holds; it doesn't mean what you were doing until today is sinful. But it might be sinful to not make some changes going forward.

A Relatively New Phenomenon

If you feel like your church hasn't historically thought much about how to reach young adults, you're not alone. For many churches, this is an area of ministry they don't have much experience in, because there simply wasn't the same need for it in the past. Young adult ministry looked really different just a few short decades ago.

A significant factor in all this is young adults are getting married later and fewer are getting married at all. In the 1960s, the median age of marriage was something like twenty-three for men and twenty-one for women. Now, on average, men are nearly thirty and women are just over twenty-seven when they get married.[3] In 1962, nearly 60 percent of people ages eighteen to thirty years old were married. Now only 20 percent of those ages eighteen to thirty are married.[4]

Young adult ministry in the '60s probably looked a lot like ministering to married people, which is where a lot of churches feel comfortable. But reaching young adults today looks like connecting with the millions of singles in their twenties and thirties. This is a significant demographic shift to absorb. Today's young adults have different needs, interests, and lifestyles, and that requires a different approach. What worked before doesn't necessarily work today.

Single for a Season, or Single for a Reason?

To reach this relatively new and rapidly growing demographic, some churches have focused on creating some form of singles ministry. I don't know about you, but the first thoughts popping in my head when I hear "singles ministry" aren't all positive. Let's play a quick word association game with singles ministry: *vibrant* or *awkward*? The problem with many singles ministries is they focus too much on being single. They have a "meat market" vibe because everyone there is trying to find a spouse, it feels uncomfortable because people who should have been asked to leave five years ago are still hanging around, and the teaching is one-dimensional because they're overaddressing singles-specific topics like loneliness and how to be content even though you're not married. They turn singleness into a problem needing to be addressed or recovered from. Focusing on the "problem" might make sense to some, but it creates a recovery group no one wants to be in for long.

For example, The Porch isn't called a "singles ministry," even though most of the people who attend are not married. It's a young adult ministry. Sure, things like dating and loneliness, and what qualities to look for in a spouse[5] are talked about, but they aren't overfocused on. As I teach young adults the full counsel of God, my goal is to equip people to grow in all aspects of their walk with Christ—not just their relationship status. It's about helping them grow into being fully mature disciples of Jesus. When I do talk about singleness, I emphasize how it's a gift,[6] not something to be recovered from. Emphasizing discipleship in all areas of life is a great way to avoid the "single for a reason" vibe permeating so many singles ministries.

Sizing Up Your Sacred Herd

Part of holding traditions loosely is being able to recognize and address your "sacred cows"—those things your church is strongly attached to and would struggle to consider changing. These could be fairly straightforward things like the style of worship music, the time and order of service, the length of the message, and so forth. But it might start to feel like meddling to examine things like the name of your church, who the pastor is, what kinds of ministries you have, the days you meet, how your leadership is structured, and whether certain people are best suited for the roles they're in.

You should not have any "sacred cows" in your ministry that are immune to examination. And you've got some work to do in culling your herd if you aren't 100 percent convinced the people who will be trusting Christ in the coming months and years would be excited to get connected at your church. Would your kids be excited to come? How about their non-Christian friends? If not, take steps to fix things. Your interest shouldn't be in keeping the herd alive but in doing whatever is necessary to maximize your impact for Christ. Bottom line: if there's a better way to do things, and the Bible gives you permission to do it, *do it*! Why wouldn't you? Be firm where Scripture is firm but flexible where Scripture is flexible. Don't be so in love with anything besides God, the Bible, and people that you aren't willing and able to change it.

Your first step on this journey is to perform a fearless self-assessment of how many sacred cows your church or ministry has. Remember, sacred cows are things you don't want to change. Measure the size of your sacred herd. Put everything on the table. What is everything that could possibly be a sacred cow? Often it's difficult to see your sacred cows, so you'll need to get some feedback—no surprise, right? *Write them all down.*

Your next step is to evaluate everything. During my time at The Porch we found it helpful to put everything into one of three buckets:

1. **Keep doing.** These things are going well, and we just need to keep up the good work.
2. **Start doing.** We aren't doing these things, but we think they are great ideas and could make us even better.
3. **Stop doing.** We need to phase out or significantly over- haul these things in order to increase our effectiveness.

Once you have everything in one of those buckets, you can actually keep, start, or stop doing the things you need to. It's especially hard to put things in the "stop" bucket, because we're naturally attached to what we've been doing. If you find you're putting a lot of things in the "keep" category, you might need to change the question to something like, "What do we want to keep doing but need to do better?" When you're bound by tradition, it's too easy to just keep doing the good things with- out ever making them the best things. Do everything you can to make what you're doing as excellent as possible.

What Young Adults Want from Church

As you're thinking about what to change, you'd probably like to know what young adults want from church. Unfortunately, the answer for nearly a full third of Millennials of what they want from church is "nothing," because they believe church is not at all important.[7] They don't want anything to do with a church because they believe they can connect with God somewhere else, because it's not relevant to them, because it's boring, because they believe God is missing from church, and because it's out-of-date. But digging deeper, it goes beyond issues of preference. Two-thirds of all Millennials believe American churchgoers are hypocrites, more than half view present-day Christianity as aggressive and critical, and nearly 50 percent believe the church is too much like an exclusive country club.[8] As you're evaluating your traditions and practices, you'll need to dig beyond things like song choice, pastoral attire, and the temperature in the sanctuary into matters of the heart and whether there are any ways your church comes across as aggressive, hypocritical, or exclusive.

One of the most important things young adults also want at church might be so obvious you'd miss it . . . other young adults! Specifically, not just other young adults attending the church but also leading the church. I've been to a lot of church leader gatherings and conferences where people have talked about how to reach young adults. One observation I've made many times is that, for more than a few of these churches, there are no young adults there as part of their teams. Is it any wonder that, if you have few or no young adults on your staff or on your stage, you might struggle to reach young adults as a church?

A Serious Leadership Challenge

As your church looks at changing traditions to reach the coming generations and increase your effectiveness for Christ, you'll need to confront this potentially unsettling reality: making your church more welcoming for the next generation of believers likely means it will become less comfortable for your current members. Are they ready for that? Are you ready for them to not be ready? Sure, you'd hope everyone would have the attitude of "We put up with anything rather than hinder the gospel of Christ" (1 Cor. 9:12), but there are probably going to be a few people—maybe a lot of people—who are attached to the traditions that need to be changed. Maybe the tradition they'd now like to change is your employment history at their church!

This will take courage. And sadly, many church leaders don't have the courage to do what needs to be done. It might not be a mystery to them what they need to do to reach young adults, but they're afraid changing things will cause the "old guard" to leave the church and take their tithes and offerings with them. This is a heart issue for those who would take offense and leave just because things are changing, but it's also a leadership issue. If the "forms" of worship just exist to meet the desires of the established and elite at your church, you have an upside-down church. Let the forms be foreign to them and familiar to the next generation of believers. You aren't called to just survive as a church until the old guard dies out; you're called to lead courageously. If your church members are not at a place to care about reaching the next generation, you have to lead them out of their spiritual narcissism and lovingly confront them with the reality that resisting change is putting their needs as believers above those of the next generation who have not yet trusted Christ. Which needs are more important?

How you communicate this matters. Be sure to not just focus on the "what" of changing traditions but also on the "why." Give your reasons, and do so with gentleness and respect. Connect what you're doing to the values you share as a church, so people can see the vision is the same while some of the details might be changing. At some point in the future, the changes you're making will need to be changed again, so don't make the specifics the entire focus.

In all this, you don't want to make it seem like you're trying to push the older and more established generations out the door. One of the most common questions I get from young adults is "Where can I find a mentor?" Young adults place a high value on learning from, interacting with, and forming connections with people from the generations before them. More than two-thirds of churched young adults say it's very important to them to receive advice from such people with similar life experiences.[9] There is absolutely room for young adults and older generations to coexist and thrive in the same church body, combining the passion and energy of the younger generation with the wisdom of the older. It's a healthy church where the younger generations honor the older ones and the older generations bless and empower the younger ones. Help your people see it's not an "us vs. them" situation but a "better together" one.

When the Challenge Is Your Leader

What if you never even get a chance to communicate the changes you'd like to make because your leader doesn't give you the approval to make any changes at all? This is also a common leadership challenge in the church—one of "leading up."

As you think and pray about communicating traditions and practices you believe need to be changed, be sure to approach this with humility and a desire to understand. Don't be a fool who only wants to speak his or her own opinions (Prov. 18:2). Don't give your answer before you've fully listened to what others have to say (v. 13). Ask questions like, "Can you help me understand this?" and "Can you tell me the history behind this?" Don't assume just because something might not be ideal for reaching young adults now it wasn't perfectly suited to reaching people when it was first put in place. It might also be accomplishing some positive outcome right now you're just not aware of.

If you're new to the church, your fresh eyes are incredibly valuable in seeing things clearly, because you won't have a "This is how we've always done it" mentality. You can help challenge assumptions and the status quo. But be mindful that tact and patience are your friends here. Write your observations down to be communicated at the right time, but don't come in guns blazing the first week or two with all the changes needing to be made. Your own "95 Theses" can wait until you fully understand the "what" and "why" of what's being done currently and you've had a chance to establish trust with your leaders.

After processing well, if you're convinced some things need to change but your leadership isn't particularly receptive, you'll need to initiate a loving and respectful conversation with them. Have an honest dialogue about the specific reasons you believe the next generation of believers would not be thrilled to connect at your church, and what you think needs to be done about it.

I can remember a time when I was struggling with this, wrestling with "what's next" for me. The Lord spoke to me at just the right time through my boss and mentor, who told our staff that when we are faced with situations where it is a challenge to "lead up" well, we should respond like these men in Scripture:

1. **Be a David.** Even when Saul was trying to kill him, David did not slander him or try to take over his place of leadership. He did not speak against the Lord's anointed (1 Sam. 24:6). No matter what kind of leader you're under, seek their good and have their best in mind. Do not speak against them. Sure, you might have to dodge a few spears, but don't let your heart turn rebellious. Seek the good of your leaders, not their overthrow.

2. **Be a Daniel.** When Daniel wanted to try a different option from what the king had planned, he first asked permission and then proposed an experiment with measurable results (Dan. 1:8–16). When you're looking to make changes your leader might not agree with, first ask their permission to try it, and then set up an experiment with clear results so you can test the idea and decide together whether it's worth pursuing further.

3. **Be a Joseph.** Joseph was faithful and excellent in every responsibility he had, whether it was running a jail (Gen. 39:20–23) or running a country (41:41). Even if the area you've been given authority over is incredibly limited, be excellent and faithful in that area and trust God's sovereignty.

Remember the Big Picture

It's great to want to have a healthy and thriving young adult population at your church, but this shouldn't be your only goal. You should want to have a healthy and thriving community of saints, some of whom are young adults. You must be committed to making your entire church all it can be, not just your ministry area. Just as it isn't about the people who have long been at your church, it also isn't only about the young adults you want to engage. You should be making room for treasures both new *and* old (Matt. 13:52).

CHAPTER 5

Under-Promise and Over-Deliver

C an Christmas help you reach young adults? I think it can, but probably not in the way you're thinking. I'm not talking about the incarnation or even the fact that people are generally more open to being invited to church around Christmastime . . . I'm talking about the movie *Elf*. In this movie, which is incredibly popular with Millennials, Will Ferrell plays Buddy, an innocent and happy-go-lucky Santa's helper who happens to end up in Manhattan. In one scene, Buddy is walking down a busy street and spots a glowing neon sign in a café window reading, "World's Best Cup of Coffee." He dashes inside and excitedly congratulates the staff, who are confused by his enthusiasm. "You did it!" he exults. "Congratulations! World's best cup of coffee! Great job, everybody. It's great to meet you!" He runs back out to the street, and eventually returns to the café with his love interest, played by Millennial actress Zooey Deschanel. He puts a blindfold on her to not ruin the surprise and urges her to take a drink of what is sure to be an incredible cup of coffee. She sips it, then tells him, "It tastes like a crappy cup of coffee." She takes the blindfold off and confirms, "It *is* a crappy cup of coffee." No, he insists, it's the world's best cup of coffee. The sign said so! But of course it isn't, and they don't go back to that café.

I've had plenty of similar experiences, and you probably have too. I remember one from before I was a Christian. I was driving around Dallas with a few of my friends one evening, looking for something fun to do. We came around a corner and saw spotlights lighting up the sky. Surely they were announcing an amazing party! We drove to where the lights were coming from and discovered it was a local club. We hustled in, ready to have the night of our lives, but when we got inside it we discovered it was empty, boring, and awful. The reason they were using all those spotlights on the outside to attract people was because there was nothing on the inside that would do the trick. We left and never went back.

Bright Lights and Cheap Cookies

I think we church leaders often do something similar in trying to reach young adults. We invest in the equivalent of bright spotlights and marketing, telling people to come to our amazing event, but then it doesn't live up to the hype. "This is going to be awesome! World-changing! Don't miss it! Bring your friends!" And then it's pretty much like any other night, except maybe with cheap pizza, some grocery store cookies, and an average band.

Nothing will make you lose trust faster with young adults than promising something you don't deliver. They've been bombarded by advertising messages since they were born. Not only do they not believe bold advertising claims but they are incredibly skeptical of the people and organizations making them. In fact, more than eight out of ten Millennials simply don't trust traditional advertising at all.[1] This means if you advertise your ministry or event as something extra special, they almost certainly will not believe you. Young adults can sense when you are trying to grow your ministry or are desperate for their presence. "Next time, come back with a friend!" That kind of neediness is not attractive. They will have a negative bias coming in the door, if they even come at all.

To Be Great, Understate

Early on at The Porch, we spent a lot of our time, energy, and resources on promotion and marketing. We told people how great it was going to be, came up with fancy graphics and handouts, and spent a lot of our time thinking about ways we could tell people about The Porch. But then we realized something: it wasn't working. People weren't coming because of things we said; they were coming because of *things their friends said.* They weren't listening to us at all when it came to marketing and promotion. We began to shift our focus from quality of promotion to quality of experience, and it made a noticeable difference. While the people coming were deaf to our promotion, they were tuned in to what was happening at The Porch each Tuesday evening. As we kept making it into something worth attending and sharing about, the people coming took care of all the marketing for us.

Instead of promotion, we started focusing on understated excellence. Our mentality became, "Even if only two people come, we are going to make the evening as excellent as we can for those two people." We knew in all likelihood that if we did our jobs well, those people would tell their friends, and it wouldn't be just two people there for long.

To be clear, though, understatement itself isn't enough to get people to attend. If you make no claims about something being great, and then it ends up not being that great, people still aren't going to come back. "No wonder they didn't say it would be awesome . . . because it wasn't." But understatement does give young adults the freedom and room to figure out for themselves what you have to offer. They can more easily decide whether or not it's something they want to keep coming back to and tell their friends about. Their "BS meter" is not triggered by any claims of awesomeness, so their impressions of the experience will end up being more positive and untainted by expectation.

There's a phrase we used often when I was part of The Porch: we wanted to "surprise and delight" the people who came. When you promote things in an understated way but then the experience turns out to be excellent, it is a delightful surprise. "Whoa—Tedashii is rapping at The Porch! Nobody said anything about this. This is awesome!" That's the kind of reaction you want. It doesn't have to be anything like bringing in a well-known Christian rapper—maybe your people wouldn't enjoy that at all. But if you can figure out how to consistently surprise and delight your attendees in both big and small ways, it builds trust and anticipation.

Kill the Hero

One of the ways we remained understated as well as set ourselves up to surprise and delight attendees was by not announcing in advance who was teaching at The Porch. It might have been me or another guy in our regular teaching rotation, it might have been Todd Wagner, who's the senior pastor of Watermark, or it might have been Francis Chan or John Piper. All of those leaders have taught at The Porch, by the way, but there wasn't a whisper of their names on our social media channels or pre-service announcements. Some people did catch wind of it and tell their friends in advance, but we didn't promote it. Or sometimes we would bring in other staff at Watermark who weren't a "big name" but would delightfully surprise everyone by how God used them to communicate truth to his people.

One of the main reasons we do this is to fight the culture of Christian celebrity that's so easy to get caught up in. We aren't trying to make anybody famous except Jesus, so we "kill the hero" if it could be confused as anybody other than him. Sure, Wagner, Piper, and Chan are going to do a great job of teaching the Word, but the One they're pointing to is Jesus, so he's who we're promoting.

I always found Todd to be world-class at cultivating a healthy culture of anti-celebrity humility for our staff, especially for those with a speaking platform onstage. He told our staff many times that one of the ministry experiences he was praying to have was for someone to invite him to Watermark. Sure, he was the founding pastor and still taught on a lot of weekends, but he said he would love nothing more than for someone familiar with our church—but not with him—to meet him randomly out in public and invite him to come and see what God was doing in our midst. In his mind this would be the ultimate test of "non-celebrity-ness." The only way Todd wanted to be recognized was as a servant of Christ and a steward of the mysteries of God (1 Cor. 4:1).

Killing the hero is something I have to do in my own heart, because my flesh craves recognition and fame. As The Porch grew, in some people's eyes (not my own, I assure you) I became something of a local celebrity. Thousands of people have seen and heard me teach, so it's not rare for me to be recognized when I'm somewhere in Dallas (it also doesn't help that I'm six foot seven). If unchecked, my ego can swell like a prideful balloon, and I have to be intentional to pop it and step off the pedestal it tries to put me on.

Not too long ago I was hanging out down by the stage after teaching at The Porch, talking with whoever came down, like we did every week. Two girls approached, and they were acting more like concertgoers than churchgoers. They looked giddy and a little nervous, and as they got near me, one of them grabbed my arm and said to her friend, "Oh my gosh, I can't believe I'm touching JP!" I felt pretty awkward—even now, writing about it is awkward and weird—but there's a part of my heart that enjoyed the recognition. I gently told the girls the way they were acting was feeding my ego in a way that wasn't healthy. I said I'd love to talk with them about Jesus and what's going on in their lives, but just as a normal guy and not like some quasi-celebrity. We ended up having a great conversation—and it wasn't about me.

A Healthy Amount of FOMO

As we practiced understatement, we also didn't mind using a little FOMO[2] to our advantage. After Francis Chan spoke at The Porch, someone who wasn't there that night later told me, "I wish I had known—I would have been there!" My response was, "You wish you'd known what? That Jesus was going to show up and move powerfully? Of course it was going to happen. It happens every week." I fully believe as we are surrendered to God, he is going to show up in big ways every week. We beg him to, and he does, time after time. I would tell people they don't want to miss The Porch any week—but it's because of what God's going to do, not because of who's got the mic.

FOMO is powerful because it creates a "you should have been there" atmosphere that people will quickly hear about from their friends who attend. This is also a result of the "surprise and delight" mindset. Young adults communicate with each other way more than any form of marketing can. When they're trying to figure out whether something is worth going to, they will hit up their friends and social networks to see what other people think. This collective word-of-mouth information is a big part of what they use to make decisions. If you deliver the goods, young adults will share it with everyone they can. If you build trust that whatever you are offering will be excellent, they will use their relational capital to invite all of their friends.

But of course, this means you have to deliver the goods. If you tell them a program or event will be excellent and then it isn't, you've lost them.

So, Is It OK to Market Anything?

My point isn't that you should never market something or tell people about what's happening and when. My point is, promotion shouldn't be your focus, and it certainly shouldn't trump execution. It's not a sin to share something coming up, but don't do it in such a way that automatically declares what you normally do isn't great.

Every week The Porch staff makes announcements of some kind to let people know what's coming up that they should know about, and uses social media pages to keep people in the loop on what is going on. For example, what's up on The Porch Facebook page right now might include a video clip from the current message series, a story of life change from a Porch volunteer, pictures of young adults worshiping and enjoying time together, and event details of a '90s-themed roller skate block party happening next month, to name a few. We shouldn't be afraid to share what's happening. But how we do it matters. Instead of telling people a message is going to be unforgettable, we can let them hear a clip so they can decide for themselves. Instead of promising they'll connect with God in a unique way, we can give them a taste of others worshiping. Instead of guaranteeing God will change their life, we can share an example of how he changed someone else's life. Instead of telling them the block party is going to be the most epic '90s party they've ever seen, we can post the details and trust people will tell their friends about it, since previous parties we've thrown have been really fun.

What You Win Them with, You Win Them To

Excellence honors God and inspires people. We should work hard as unto the Lord (Col. 3:23) and do our best to stay relevant and innovative to reach as many people as possible (1 Cor. 9:22). As you try to make your experiences excellent, keep in mind what you win someone *with*, you win them *to*. If you rely solely on a high-quality worship production, polished transitions, and tastefully humorous, relatable, and time-boxed messages to attract and retain people, they'll stick around for as long as you keep offering that or until they find somewhere else doing it better. Or maybe they'll just put you on their rotation of similar churches they hang out at, so you'll see them every month or two. There's nothing wrong with a polished service production; it just can't be the *main* thing.

What Young Adults Want from Church

So, what are young adults looking for at church? If it's a good idea to under-promise and over-deliver, what are you supposed to deliver? The point of this entire book is to help answer this question, so a lot of these points and more are further unpacked in other chapters, but here are a few things that stand out from my own years of experience as well as research others have done. If you focus on these things, they will go a long way toward "delivering" what young adults want and need from church.

Authenticity

Young adults want a church that's real. They want you to be who you are, not some dressed-up version of the perfect Christian. They want to know where you struggle. They want to be able to relate to your flaws. They want you to be transparent. They want you to have high character, but you'd better not be faking it.

Connection with Jesus

Young adults want to know who the real Jesus is. They want to have a personal and vibrant relationship with him. They don't need to hear about a cosmic buddy, or a genie who will give them a better life, or even someone who thinks they're really special. They want their hearts to be captured by a loving and holy God.

Meaningful Relationships

Young adults crave community. They want a chance to connect deeply with others. They want to do life with other believers. They want to meet like-minded people as well as those who are different from them. They want to build close personal friendships.

Cultural Discernment

Young adults want to know what the Bible says, what it means, and how it applies to them here and now. They want to be able to positively engage with and contribute to culture and society. They want to stay relevant and engaged in what's happening in their world. They want to have solid answers for the questions they and others are asking.

Mission and Vision

Young adults want to understand their purpose in life. They want to know how to discover and use their gifts. They want to be reminded and inspired by how and why their faith matters. They want to serve the world around them, be fully deployed, and have meaningful responsibility. They don't want to wait "until they grow up" to do what God has called them to do.

Discipleship

Young adults want to grow in their faith. They want opportunities to learn and be challenged. They want to be mentored. They want to understand how their vocation and calling fit into a life of worship.

A Promise I Can Actually Make

I promise that you don't need a certain budget, facility, or staff to pull this off. None of the things I just talked about are specific to a particular church model or denomination. All of them do, however, require a commitment to learning about this generation and engaging them in a way that delivers more than you promised. Oh, and don't forget to provide the world's best coffee.

CHAPTER 6

Define a Path Forward

F orget real estate. You can't afford it anyway."
That's the headline of a new Monopoly game I saw the other day. I'm not much of a Monopoly guy myself, but it's one of the most popular board games of all time, and there are a lot of different versions of the classic. Oh, Star Wars is your thing? How about the Simpsons? Or maybe national parks, or Disney? Yup, there's a Monopoly for that.

And now there's the latest edition: Monopoly for Millennials. Because "Adulting is hard" and "You deserve a break from the rat race" (quotes from the back of the box), the game is all about collecting experiences instead of properties. After all, experiences last forever, and what Millennial has enough money for a down payment anyway? In the game you can surf your friend's couch, visit the vegan bistro, or head out on a meditation retreat. And whoops, your web-streaming service free trial just expired, so go ahead and pay the bank $40. On the cover, Rich Uncle Pennybags is taking a selfie of himself sporting Ray-Bans, earbuds, a to-go coffee . . . and of course he has a participation medal pinned to his chest. The game pieces include hashtags and emojis instead of top hats and old cars. It's actually kind of genius how many Millennial stereotypes Hasbro was able to fit into the game.

Walmart was the first store to sell it, initially priced at $19.82 (a clever shout-out to the first birth year of the Millennial generation by some accounts), but they sold out pretty quickly. Units started selling for two to three times that on eBay. Reaction to the game, just like to the Millennial music video we made, was immediate, immense, and mixed. The online reviews range from "Upsetting Millennials is reason enough to own this game" to "I would give this no stars if I could." There were a lot more negative reviews, but plenty I couldn't quote in a Christian book. It's safe to say Millennials felt pretty strongly about how the game portrayed their generation.

The American (Bad) Dream

The game of Monopoly is all about achieving the American Dream of owning real estate and getting as much money as you can. The person with the most at the end wins. I think one of the reasons Millennials reacted so strongly to this version of the game is because they see it as mockingly stereotyping how the American Dream is slipping through their generation's fingers. The classic vision of owning a home, becoming debt-free, retiring comfortably, and pursuing one's passions feels less and less realistic for today's young adults. Nearly half of them believe the American Dream is now unattainable.[1] They're not sure where they're heading or what their goals should be. Many young adults are unsure of how to navigate finances and their future, to say nothing of faith, friendships, anxiety, depression, a host of other issues, and of course making the big decisions that will define the rest of their lives. What does a life well lived even look like anymore? Where should they turn for answers? What should they be dreaming about attaining? What's the right path forward?

You can help young adults answer these questions. Scratch that—you *must* help young adults answer these questions.

This isn't to say you become a "helicopter pastor" who holds their hands, makes decisions for them, and shelters them from the consequences of real-life choices for the next twenty years— Millennials got enough of this from their own parents. But as a minister of the gospel (and I mean this in a 1 Peter 2:9 kind of way that applies to every Christian, not just those getting a paycheck from a church), you have the words and wisdom of Jesus, the words of eternal life (John 6:68). Surely those words from God's Word can help the next generation chart a course through life. Just like the original young adult disciples said to Jesus, where else could they go?

A Path Forward in Your Ministry

I got to write a book called *Welcome to Adulting* not too long ago—my first shot at the published author thing. That book is all about helping young adults define a path forward for their lives as they navigate faith, friendships, finances, and their future. It's basically The Porch in book form, with teaching, stories, and advice from the hundreds of messages and blogs we'd created over the years, drawn from more than a decade of young adult ministry as well as from my own experience as a Millennial. I wrote it speaking directly to young adults, but my hope is it could also be helpful to people like you, who want to minister to and lead young adults. I'll touch on some similar points here, but that book has a lot I won't be able to cover.

One quick aside: as you think about helping young adults define a path forward in their lives, you'll also want to spend some time thinking about their path forward into your ministry and church. For example, how will they hear about it to know it exists? What will their experience of parking and being greeted be like? Who's going to engage with them, and how? How will you share the gospel with them and answer any questions they have? Where do first-timers go? How do people get more information on what's going on and how to get more involved? How do—and should they—join a small group, join the church, start serving, and so on? You get what I'm saying.

The Porch has its own methods for all of those things, but that's just what works for that particular ministry; they aren't necessarily a prescription for how you have to do it. Where there are applicable general principles, I'll try to mention them. One of the main things we always tried to keep in mind and build into our ministry is that there should be clear connections and handoff points between someone's stages of involvement. Things should flow and make sense from one step to the next. We should try to proactively answer for attendees and participants, "What's my next step, and when/how do I take it?"

Discipleship: The Real Path Forward

The real path forward I'm talking about is much bigger than how to get connected into a ministry or church. It's about how to take the next steps in the abundant life God offers, and how to connect with God and with his people. It's about how to help young adults become disciples—fully devoted followers of Christ—in their twenties and thirties. It's about replacing the American Dream with a much bigger and better vision.

There's so much that could be included on this topic, way more than I have room for in this chapter or even in this book. People a lot smarter than me have written thousands of pages on how to follow God, grow in your relationship with him, and become more like Jesus. For the purpose of leading Millennials, though, I'd like to touch on some of the topics I think are most relevant to today's young adults.

If having a structure helps, let's do it like this:

Decision-making

Income and money

Singleness

Community and friendships

Isolation and anxiety

Passions and work

Love and dating

Ends of the earth

This chapter will just be the "CliffsNotes" versions of how we talked about these things at The Porch and how I covered them in *Welcome to Adulting*, but you'll get an idea of how to address each topic and define a path forward for your attendees and listeners.

Decision-Making

When I talk with young adults after I teach a message, I often get asked "What should I do in this situation?" kinds of questions. Young adults are facing a lot of decisions, and they're looking for reliable places to get answers. Sometimes the answers are clear in Scripture, other times they are gray areas Scripture speaks to, and many times they are purely "right or left, not right or wrong" situations. For decisions in the third category especially, young adults need a framework for decision-making that is rooted in Scripture but doesn't prescribe a particular answer. One of my fellow pastors at Watermark put these ten questions together from the wisdom of the Proverbs, and I think they're perfect for discipling young adults in *how* to make decisions, not just *what* to decide.[2]

1. Do I have all the facts? (Prov. 18:13, 17)
2. Am I fully entrusting this decision to the Lord? (Prov. 3:5–6; 16:3; 28:25)
3. Is the pressure of time forcing me to make a premature decision I might not otherwise make? (Prov. 19:2; 21:5; 25:8)
4. For better or worse, what are the possible motives that could be driving this decision? (Prov. 16:2; 20:9; 21:2)

5. How should my past experiences inform this decision? (Prov. 17:10; 26:11)

6. What is the collective counsel of my community? (Prov. 12:15; 15:22; 20:18)

7. Have I honestly considered the warning signs? (Prov. 10:17; 16:25; 27:6)

8. Have I fully considered all the possible outcomes for each course of action I'm considering? (Prov. 14:1, 15, 23; 27:12)

9. Could this decision jeopardize my integrity or hinder my witness for the Lord in any way? (Prov. 10:9; 20:7; 22:1; 25:26)

10. Is there a better option that would allow me to make a greater impact for God's kingdom? (Prov. 11:30)

Income and Money

My first job after technical college was managing an Abercrombie & Fitch store in Dallas. Yeah, I know . . . *#goals*. It paid $23,000 a year, which felt like a fortune after making about $5,000 a year working part-time in school. Of course it didn't feel that way for long—there was too much I wanted to buy. I changed jobs a lot, chasing the dollar. But it was never enough. Even when I eventually got a job paying ten times as much as I made working at Abercrombie (not my pastoring job, by the way), I still wanted more.

Money is a huge focus for today's young adults, and they have this intense mix of big dreams and big debts. Just over half of Millennials expect to eventually become millionaires (don't ask me how).[3] And they'll need those millions to pay off their debts, since Millennials hold more than *$1 trillion* of America's $3.6 trillion in consumer debt.[4] Overall, Millennials are less well-off than members of earlier generations were at the same ages, with lower earnings, fewer assets, and less wealth.[5]

The real problem with Millennials and money, though, isn't their debt—it's the myth they've believed, along with just about everyone else. The myth is having more money will make them happy. Your job is to help redefine their goals and lay out a healthy path forward with money.

You might feel funny talking to young adults about money—like, shouldn't you be focusing on something more spiritual? Tell that to Jesus, who talked more about money than any other topic and who said the location of your money is a great indicator of how your heart's doing (Matt. 6:21; Luke 12:34).

Here are a few of the ways we addressed money at The Porch:

- *Money isn't a measure of worth.* Our world talks about "net worth." But money isn't a measure of a person's value, it's just a measure of the value of what they possess. Young adults need to know they are priceless, no matter how much money they do or don't have.

- *Money isn't success.* When young adults tell me they want to be successful, they often mean they want to make a lot of money. But success just means they accomplished their goals, whatever those were. What about important goals like raising godly kids or sharing the gospel? People can be really successful at collecting green-tinged portraits of dead presidents, or they can be really successful at something that truly matters. It's hard to do both (Matt. 6:24).

- *Money isn't security.* It's wise to be prepared for the unexpected, but saving money becomes a problem when it's done to the extreme or for the wrong reasons. It can quickly turn into an idol, causing people to trust in money for security rather than trusting in God. Money isn't trustworthy, but God is.

- *Money isn't evil.* Money itself is not evil. It's morally neutral and can be used for either good or evil. The same money could be used to feed a hungry child or feed an unhealthy addiction. And that's why the *love* of money is a root of all kinds of evil: it affects what people do with money, and what they are willing to do to get money.

- *It isn't your money.* Young adults have no money. And that's not a comment about stagnant wages or crushing debt—all money is ultimately God's money. As with every resource on this earth, God created it and gave it to them to steward during their lifetimes. Anyone think they earned it? Well, who made them, gave them their gifts and abilities, allowed them to be born where and when they were, and led them to find the opportunities they've found? Yup, God. Treat money like it's his, because it is.

- *Principles of money management.* We also talked about practical things like living below your means, being wary of debt in general, avoiding credit card debt like the plague, having a budget, buying less stuff, buying experiences vs. things, being generous, and storing up treasure in heaven.

Singleness

Ah, singleness . . . the elephant in the room of just about every young adult ministry. Statistically, most young adults you interact with will get married someday. But it doesn't mean everyone will. Some will choose not to get married because they don't have the desire to (they might possess the often-misunderstood "gift of singleness,"[6] or they might just be selfish). But some people who *do* want to get married will still end up never taking a step into marriage. And to those people, I'd encourage you to say it's OK. Not just it's *going* to be OK, like someday they'll be in heaven and won't lament their past singleness on earth. No, it is OK *right now*. There are lots of things they should be doing to take advantage of their singleness, like getting to know the Bible better and building healthy habits.[7]

It may not seem to them like it's OK. It may seem like they're missing out and their lives won't be complete. But marriage is not the main goal of life. Marriage doesn't make anyone complete. And being single doesn't mean they are somehow damaged goods. Jesus was single, and he was perfect. The apostle Paul was also single, and he taught that staying single was a pretty good idea (1 Cor. 7:8).

After all, marriage does not automatically make someone happier. There are benefits to being married, and the same goes for being single.[8] There are also downsides to both. The right path forward for young adults, whether they find themselves single or married, is to make the most of what they have and strive to be content (Phil. 4:11–13).

Community and Friendships

Today's young adults are the most connected generation in history because of technology. But they're also some of the loneliest, with many of them having no close relationships.[9]

The path forward here is not just to have friends. It's to have people in their lives who are what I like to call "community." What does that mean? A Christian community is a group of people who are committed to being part of each other's lives and seeking what's best for one another, no matter what. They care enough to speak the truth, even if the truth is hard to receive, and they love enough to give tough love if it's needed.

I've heard it said that a friend is someone who will come bail you out of jail, while a best friend is someone who is sitting beside you in the cell. If that's the illustration, then your community would be the ones who did everything they could to keep you out of jail by dealing with the pattern of bad decisions or habits they saw might put you there eventually. If you still ended up in jail, they'd come visit and bail you out if needed. But they also might purposefully *not* bail you out if in wisdom they all agreed it would be in your best interest to face the consequences. They'd stick with you through it all, but they wouldn't enable you or encourage you to make bad choices.

These are the kinds of biblical friends young adults need . . . not the Facebook kind.

Isolation and Anxiety

The loneliness and lack of community I just talked about lead many young adults to isolate themselves and pursue their own desires—an unwise move according to God (Prov. 18:1). As a result, many young adults are incredibly stressed and anxious about all sorts of things, with no one to help them work through these issues. According to the World Health Organization, America is the most anxious country they've evaluated.[10] Within our worried country, young adults are the most anxious of everyone; more than 50 percent of Millennials have lost sleep in the past month because of stress.[11] Anxiety is the number one topic I was asked to teach about at The Porch.

I've personally experienced panic attacks in the middle of the night. I've been faced with racing thoughts and have even sought medical help in a season of severe anxiety. I've continued to return to the truths of God's Word and have found the most freedom in simple ideas I've been skeptical of in the past.

Your job is to give young adults principles that can help point them back to truth and ultimately to hope. The root of anxiety is a lack of trust in the One who is in control. The solution is to help young adults get to know him and learn to trust him more. You have to help them fight the two lies at the root of worry: God is not in control, and God is not good. If they trust that God is in control and he has their best interests in mind, they won't have anything to worry about.

Consider this equation: God is in control + God is good + God loves you = Your peace. This is the path forward.[12]

Passions and Work

After my job at Abercrombie, I took a job selling gym memberships because I found out I wasn't passionate about retail clothing. Then I went into graphic design, and then telecommunications, and then IT consulting. I found out I wasn't passionate about any of those things. Let's just say I had quite the roundabout journey to becoming a pastor (more on this in the next chapter).

A lot of young adults today have similar stories to mine. They're looking for their dream job—an elusive unicorn of an occupation that uses their skills, gives them meaningful work, and allows them to live without financial worries. It's pretty hard to find, so this generation is known for job-hopping around, looking for the perfect fit. These days, 90 percent of Millennials expect to stay in a job for a maximum of three years.[13]

I think a big reason for this is they've been given some really, really bad advice in this area. And it's this: "follow your passions." Everywhere young adults turn, they're being told to follow their passions. And they're listening. In fact, their number one characteristic of a dream job is to feel passionate about it.[14]

This is also pretty much the opposite of what the Bible teaches. We're not supposed to follow our passions; we're supposed to bring our passions under control (Gal. 5:24). Instead of following our hearts (Jer. 17:9), we're called to follow God and to become passionate about what he's passionate about.

Does that mean you should be telling young adults to work at a job they're not passionate about? Maybe. It depends on the situation. If they have a job they are passionate about, that's great. Tell them to work hard at it. But if they can't find a job like that, or they already have a job they're not passionate about—well, they still need to work (Prov. 14:23; 2 Thess. 3:10). So encourage them to work hard at whatever job they have as a great employee. I encourage young adults to try to be God's perfect provision for the job they have instead of looking for the perfect job somewhere else.

Love and Dating

In a ministry with thousands of young adults coming every week, there's going to be some dating going on. There's probably going to be some love too, followed by more than a few marriages. Finding a spouse—or at least not being alone—was definitely one of the biggest "felt needs" I observed in our Porch attendees.

Dating looks different now than it used to. Online dating has become the norm, with the internet being the number one place singles met their first date last year, according to Match .com's 2018 "Singles in America" study.[15] Online dating caters to every kind of preference—there are sites for Christians, Jews, Muslims, Trump supporters, people who self-select as intelligent, and vegans. There's also BikerKiss ("Two wheels, two hearts, one road"), FarmersOnly ("Single in the country"), and The Ugly Bug Ball ("Dating for the aesthetically average"). The idea with all these is not to appeal to the most people but to find—or be found by—the right person.

And who is this "right person"? Is the mythical "one" out there? My favorite answer to the question of "How do I know if I've found 'the one'?" is, "You married them. Next question?"

Of course, there's more to it, but the point is "the one" doesn't exist. There isn't a single person out there who is your soul mate just waiting to be discovered. I'm convinced there are other guys who would have made a better match for my wife, Monica. But she chose me, I chose her, and we're in this till death do us part. We became each other's "one" when we got married.

The right path forward for young adults isn't to look for "the one" but to try to *become* the type of person the one they're looking for would be looking for, to paraphrase Andy Stanley.[16] And to look for the type of person God tells them to look for. For guys, it's a woman who is trustworthy, modest, peaceful, diligent, compassionate, respectful, submissive to authority, responsible, wise, and committed to Christ.[17] For gals, it's a man who is submissive to authority, honest, kind, selfless, patient, courageous, gentle, diligent, faithful, and committed to Christ.[18]

If young adults find that person and pursue them, there are pitfalls to counsel them to avoid in dating, like dating just for fun, focusing on the physical, "trying before you buy" sexually, living together, treating love as a feeling, and thinking marriage will solve all of their problems. And of course there's the first problem to overcome—never asking someone out (looking at the guys here).[19]

Leading up to the first date, it's important to make it clear that it is, in fact, a date. After that, steer clear of the pitfalls above, be intentional, communicate clearly, and either keep dating or don't—but don't let it remain a mystery either way.

And then? If they're both fully committed to Christ, are willing to commit fully to one another, and have the blessing of other committed believers in their lives—see you at the altar.[20]

Ends of the Earth

Instead of digging into another specific topic potentially relevant to young adults, I want to remind you that the goal of defining a path forward for young adults is not to just help them *know more* from the Bible but to *do more* with what they know. This process of maturing will take time, and their progress will probably not be linear. But application is everything (James 1:22).

And beyond even that, the point of discipleship isn't just to be a disciple of Jesus but to make other disciples of Jesus (Matt. 28:19–20). This is what changes the world. And it's really just a three-step process:

1. **Be changed yourself.** Know Jesus, love Jesus, and follow Jesus.

2. **Invest deeply in a small number of people.** You don't need to have an audience of thousands, you just need a few faithful people (2 Tim. 2:2).

3. **Encourage those few people to repeat the process with others.** If you were to invest deeply in just two people for a year, and then each of them did the same thing while you did that with another two the following year, every human being on the planet would be discipled in just about two decades.[21]

And there we go—world changed.

SECTION THREE

Deploy

CHAPTER 7

Find Leaders

I f the next key leader of your ministry was drunk right now, it wouldn't surprise me at all. Before explaining what I mean, let me tell you about a few of my friends.

The professional partier. Larry[1] was what we call a "Johnny Dallas," the stereotypical worldly Dallas young adult. He helped people get drunk and high for a living. His full-time job was to throw these huge epic parties in clubs and bars, where hundreds of people would come to drink, party, and hook up. He would rent out the entire place, and they were just crazy scenes of debauchery. He thought he was living the life, drinking deep from everything the world offered—limo rides to the next scene, bottle service in the top clubs, sex with beautiful women, money, and pleasure. While he was in the middle of this lifestyle, one of his friends invited him to The Porch. Larry came and sat in the back, still high, and listened to the message. Something resonated with him, and the Holy Spirit moved in his life. Larry was invited to a Bible study, which he started attending. As he got started, he said he was cool with Jesus, as long as he didn't have to give up weed and girls. This changed as Larry continued to grow in his faith and became a follower of Christ.

As he kept growing, Larry came to us and said he wanted to serve at The Porch. He asked me what I wanted him to do. "Do you want me to be an usher or greeter or something?" "No, I don't." "I don't know what I can do for God," he said. "I don't really have any skills in that area." "Well, where do you have skills?" "I throw great parties." "Perfect! Throw great parties!" So Larry stopped throwing parties for the world and started throwing parties for the church. And thousands of young adults started coming! We called it Porch Late Night. They were pretty awesome parties, since Larry was a pro. He took his gifts and talents and started using them for God's glory. He joyfully set aside weed to lead others to the Holy Spirit. He traded womanizing for a thriving marriage.

The radio tower climber. Here's a quick one. Alex had an alcohol problem too. One day he thought it would be a good idea to climb a radio tower in just his underwear while he was drunk. *Why not?* Unfortunately for him, the local TV station thought his good idea would make a great news story, and they put his foolishness on the air. Alex's boss saw the clip but was not entertained. When Alex got to work the next day, he was fired on the spot. He got invited to The Porch, stumbled into the place hung over, got discipled, and went on to become one of our best Porch team leaders.

The karma-based workaholic. Saanvi grew up in a loving Hindu home believing in karma—the good or bad things you do determine what happens in this life and the next. Her parents were honest and generous, but her family always seemed to be going through some kind of hardship. That was OK—she didn't know exactly who God was, but she believed he would fix everything because they were trying to be good. But it didn't happen. After a heartbreaking realization in college that hard things kept happening to her family even though they tried to be good, she was pretty much done with God.

She moved to Dallas after college for a job and jumped into a relationship, but the guy ended up breaking her heart. Everything fell apart again. A friend invited her to The Porch, where Saanvi was reminded God can use suffering to draw us closer to him. A Porch volunteer named Lisa met with her every week for months, encouraging her to follow Jesus with her whole heart. Saanvi joined a women's community group, but she was more focused on her career and finding a spouse than her spiritual development, and she was still coming up empty.

And then one Easter something happened. She confessed her double life to her community group, and they reminded her of what Jesus did for her on the cross and that there is no condemnation for those who are in Christ Jesus. As she understood God's unconditional love for the first time, everything changed. Saanvi eventually started serving at The Porch, and she became one of our most faithful leaders, pouring into young adults every week for years.

The divorcée who had an abortion. And then there was this other girl, Amy. She stumbled into the ministry in a similar way to how I did. She was also a partier. She'd been divorced. She was invited, she came, and she started to grow in her faith. People could see she was different from her old self, so she had many chances to share her story. But there was something she held back. She'd had an abortion. She wasn't sure people in the church would still love her if they knew. But one day, through the movement of the Holy Spirit and the preaching of the gospel, she had the urge to tell someone she'd had an abortion. And God did the most amazing thing around her. Other girls who heard that started saying, "Me too. I thought I'd never tell anybody, but because you had the courage to speak up, I have the courage to speak up." They started to find forgiveness and healing. God used Amy's story to fuel an abortion recovery ministry bringing Christ-centered freedom to women who felt trapped by their secret sin.[2] Amy became a Porch leader, then she served on our full-time staff leading the women of The Porch. Now she's married and a full-time mom, but it hasn't stopped her from telling everyone who will listen about how Jesus changed her life.

Don't Be Discouraged

As I tell you to "find leaders," this might be another eye-roll moment for you. "I'd love to find some leaders, JP, but all I see around me are people who need to be led, not people who are qualified to lead." Well, they might not be leaders *yet*, but that doesn't mean God doesn't have some incredible plans to raise up leaders in your midst. It's easy to get discouraged about the future of your ministry if you don't see leadership potential all around you, but you must remember the gospel has the power to completely transform people. That's my story and the story of so many young adults who have been incredible leaders in our ministry. Oh, and how about Paul and Peter (Acts 9:1–19)? How long did it take for them to become effective ministry leaders? The leaders in your ministry might not come from the current Christian ministry subculture you're living in. These future leaders may very well still be pagans, waiting to hear the gospel message and be discipled. God loves to turn the licentious into leaders in his church.

Why Does This Matter?

If you don't bring leaders into your ministry, its potential will be capped by your capacity and capabilities. You might be a gifted leader yourself, but you have limits. These limits might be in your wiring or leadership style, or might be as simple as your limited margin. You have the same twenty-four hours in a day as everyone else, and that's it. You cannot—and should not—be shouldering all the leadership responsibilities in your ministry. And if you are, you might be able to handle it all now, sure, but what if your ministry grows? Will you still be able to maintain your current level of involvement and contribution? It would not be healthy to do so. Or let's just talk about the future. The cold, hard reality is you won't be around forever. If the leadership stops when you stop, the ministry stops. Finding leaders is a way to sustain the health of your ministry over the long term. You should be looking to eventually replace yourself by pouring into the current and future leaders of your ministry now.

During my time at The Porch we followed the "Exodus 18 model" (Exod. 18:13–26) extensively as a church. If you're not immediately familiar with what I mean, it comes from the time when Moses led the people of Israel out of Egypt. Moses was providing leadership, making decisions, and solving problems for the people from morning until evening, every day. Sounds exhausting! His father-in-law saw this and told Moses something like, "Son, you're going to burn out. You need to get some people to help you lead." He told Moses to appoint trustworthy leaders under him who could lead the people in just about every area, involving Moses only when the issues were particularly significant. Moses took this advice, and it went well for him.

If I had been the only one leading at The Porch, it would not have been a healthy ministry—and it probably would've fit in my living room. I didn't have enough capacity to lead two-hundred-plus volunteers, let alone the thousands of people who came every week. But we appointed "leaders of leaders" to do much of the work of the ministry, and we were healthier for it. We'll talk more in another chapter about giving the ministry away to your leaders. But in order to give your leaders responsibility, you first have to find them.

Are They out There?

The leaders you need are out there. They are people with followers and influence yet to be leveraged for the kingdom. They are people with leadership potential that just hasn't been tapped yet. They might not be in your ministry, or you just might not have realized they already are. I have had bankers, teachers, doctors, entrepreneurs, retail clerks, mathematicians, salespeople, nurses, mechanics, consultants, and many more who led and served with me. They work hard in their craft "as working for the Lord, not for human masters" (Col. 3:23), but their passion has been redirected from their profession to their purpose—to know Jesus and make him known. I've heard this so many times from people I served with: "I've never felt so alive." And my response is always the same: "That's because for the first time you're living as you were intended to."

I fully believe working hard at a profession can be worship that honors God and serves as a platform for witnessing (1 Pet. 2:12), but the truth is work has become an idol to many. Corporate America and the financial success it promises is exploiting many of the people who might otherwise be leading in your ministry, selling them the American Dream in exchange for their souls. That's not a good trade—offer them a better one! Young adults desperately want to be part of something that matters. Their jobs are not the ultimate expression of their calling,[3] and less than one-third of Millennials are deeply engaged at work emotionally and behaviorally.[4] Call them to more. Call them to something they can give themselves fully to. This doesn't mean they need to quit their jobs and become full-time church staff . . . but it might.

Call People to Become Leaders

My own call to ministry was exactly that—a phone call. My story was similar to Alex's and Larry's. I loved the world, someone invited me to church, I began to wrestle with who God is, and then Jesus became my greatest affection.

I was working in business development in corporate America, and as I fell deeper in love with Jesus, I began to see my workplace as a mission field. Every day became more and more about ministry. One day I came home exhausted, and Monica, my wife, asked if it had been a difficult day at work. I realized I had not done much for the company I worked for. My customers were happy, my sales were happening, but much of my time was spent ministering to those around me. I started my day studying the Bible in a discipleship group, I met with a guy over lunch who was considering leaving his wife, I read several apologetic articles, and I shared the gospel with some coworkers.

I had heard "You should only do ministry if you can't do anything else." I thought it meant "You should only do ministry if you're not gifted at anything else." But I realized now it meant to only do ministry if you're so consumed with ministry that you're not very effective at anything else.

The next day I went to work, and as I sat at my desk, I heard what I now believe was the voice of God. He said, *You're going to work for me.* It startled my soul. I left the office at 1:30 in the afternoon and begged my friend Brandon to leave work early and meet me at my house. He did. It was about 2:30 when we met, and I told him I thought I had been called into vocational ministry. I didn't know what to do, so I went online, got an attorney, and began to start a 501(c)(3)—all before 2:45 p.m. Brandon encouraged me to stop and pray. He said, "If God called you into ministry, he's going to show you his plan in his timing." This made sense to me, so I took a week to pray. Every day I prayed, "God, put me where you want me and help me find contentment there."

On the fifth day, as I was walking through the foyer of the company I worked for, my phone rang. It was a man who had discipled me at Watermark. He said, "I have a job I want you to consider." I thought he needed me to volunteer somewhere, and I was ready to serve. He clarified, however, that he was talking about a staff position at the church. I was so confused. I started to tell him how I had not gone to seminary, as if he didn't know (when we first met, I didn't know the Old Testament from the New Testament). Then, all of a sudden, I thought I realized what was going on. "Oh, you talked to Brandon?" "Brandon who?" he responded. He had not talked to anyone. The Lord put my name on his heart as he read an open job description. He knew I was underequipped, and he knew it would mean a significant pay cut for me, but he didn't say my no for me. He took a risk and picked up the phone. And my life would never be the same.

Make bold requests in calling people to lead. Don't be afraid to recruit gifted people. You never know how God might want to use them. Call them to invest in something significant! Ask them to think about where they can have the most impact on things that will matter one hundred or one thousand years from now. This is just following Jesus's example in calling fishermen to be fishers of people (Matt. 4:19).

It could start as simply as, "Would you pray about something with me?" This is what I said to my friend Luke a few years ago while we were walking through a Haitian village on an international discipleship trip. At the time we were looking to fill a full-time staff position in our young adult small groups ministry. Luke had an MBA and was working for a top-tier management consulting firm, traveling extensively, and making six figures. He had been serving at The Porch for a few months, and I had no idea if he was looking for a career change. He'd never told me he was being called to ministry. So I decided to start the conversation and see where God took it. As it turned out, God used it to call Luke to leave the consulting world, take a significant pay cut, and come on full-time staff a few months later! When he was a year or so into the job, I asked Luke to summarize how he felt about his transition. He told me, "Two words: no regrets." It started with a simple but bold request. Eventually Luke was leading all of the operations at Watermark. He was even more gifted than I had presumed and even a bigger blessing than I would have guessed. I'm glad God had me ask him a question.

Use Leaders to Help Find Leaders

If you shoulder the burden of finding leaders all by yourself, it can feel overwhelming. You probably don't know every person who's a potential leader in your ministry. Use other people to help you. Existing leaders are one of the best sources of new leaders. During my time at The Porch, one of the responsibilities of every volunteer team leader was to replace themselves. This doesn't mean we wanted them to stop serving as soon as possible; it means we wanted them to help select, train, and disciple the person who would be taking their place whenever God moved them on to what he had next for them.

There's a former Porch leader named Keith whom I often referred to as "The best Porch leader we've ever had." He led his team with excellence and care, but the main reason I say that is because Keith had a guy named Ryan on his team (you'll hear more about Ryan later). Keith recognized Ryan's leadership gifts and vision and saw Ryan would do an incredible job of leading the team. Keith made a point of raising Ryan up as the next team leader, but he didn't just hand over the reins and then stop serving when we made Ryan's leadership role official. He believed strongly enough in Ryan's leadership that he stayed on the team, happily serving under Ryan. Keith modeled vision and humility in how he transitioned leadership to Ryan, and it's an example I've never forgotten.

If you have people already leading and serving in your ministry, use them to help you find the next generation of leaders. In my experience, the number one source of solid new volunteers is recommendations from current volunteers. Don't let a leader leave without speaking into who should come after them and ideally pouring into that person as well.

I'd summarize it this way: ask people you know and trust to help you find potential leaders they know and trust.

Build Leaders

It might not be obvious right away when someone has leadership potential. They might not even be a Christian yet. Or they might not be mature enough to take on a position of leadership. Don't make that person a leader too quickly (1 Tim. 5:22). Instead, focus on helping them develop as a servant and follower of Jesus, and give them leadership responsibility when they're ready for it. (Sidenote: they might not always *feel* ready for it, so your job may be to encourage them to step out in faith and help them navigate the journey into leadership. Do not overlook those who are willing to lead, even if they aren't quite ready to lead yet.)

At The Porch, we didn't have a complicated leadership development system. There was a little bit of classroom time for new volunteers (more on this later), but almost all leadership training was "on the job." We'd focus on spending quality time with our current and potential leaders, involving them in as many real-life ministry situations as possible, and consistently emphasizing leadership principles and vision. Our general rule was experienced leaders should always involve someone less experienced in meetings and pastoral care situations. This way the other person could see and learn how something was done, growing in their ability to lead in the future.

Part of the reason The Porch can have a simpler leadership development model is because it is a ministry of a local church, and all its volunteers and leaders are committed members of Watermark. Much of what contributes to the development and maturity of Porch leaders and volunteers comes as they live out the covenant[5] they've made, such as:

- maintaining a growing personal relationship with Jesus (John 15:5);
- submitting to the leadership and authority of biblically qualified elders (Heb. 13:17);
- connecting regularly and deeply in community with other Christians for Bible study, prayer, accountability, and fellowship (Heb. 10:24–25); and
- learning to resolve conflict well (Matt. 18:15–17).[6]

Those things are foundational to someone being ready for leadership. If a person is a fully devoted follower of Christ, they are a potential leader, whether it's in a one-talent or a ten-talent capacity (Matt. 25:14–30). If you help people grow in their relationship with Jesus, their leadership potential will grow as well.

The Peter Principle

Let me offer one important clarification before we move on. It's important for someone to have some leadership capacity and gifts. Though anyone can be a leader in some way, Scripture says some people are especially gifted for it (Rom. 12:8). You need to be careful to not raise someone up to a point where their leadership responsibilities exceed their leadership capacities. In business, this is known as the Peter Principle,[7] which says people tend to rise in an organization to the point of their incompetence and then become ineffective. This happens because good performance in one job does not guarantee the ability to perform strongly in another.

I learned this lesson fairly early in my ministry with The Porch. As we were picking leaders for Porch teams, the main criteria I was using was faithfulness. Was a person committed to the ministry? Were they showing up every week and doing everything asked of them? Did they love God? Were they trustworthy? If so, they were leadership material. So I looked around and found one of our most faithful volunteers, and I asked him to lead a team. This should have gone great, because he was all those things I mentioned—committed, faithful, trustworthy, and so on. There was just one problem—he wasn't a great leader! His personality and gifts were perfect for serving on a team but not for leading a team. He didn't enjoy being a leader, and the team didn't thrive under his leadership. I had promoted him to a leadership role that exceeded his leadership gifts, and it wasn't good for anyone. We talked it through together, found another leader to replace him, and watched him thrive again as a faithful member of the team.

What Does a Leader Do?

I've had multiple leaders and volunteers tell me they've learned more about leadership from serving at The Porch than they did in school or at their jobs, and it's prepared them for life in a way few other things have. Above all else, that's the work of God in their life, but I believe he's used some of these leadership principles we have consistently emphasized with our leaders and volunteers to grow them in this way.

- The first responsibility of a leader is to **define reality**. The last is to say thank you. In between, a leader is a servant. Leaders lead by serving; they also serve by leading. As a leader, it's important to prioritize others' needs by serving them and also to take ownership and initiative.
- A leader's role is to **unleash** the leaders on your team (10 percent), **encourage** the followers on your team with vision (80 percent), and **challenge** the stagnant on your team to walk in faithfulness (10 percent).
- To lead others well, leaders must **lead themselves well and live as examples**. Know what you are good at and capitalize on those strengths. Know where you are

weak and get people around you who are good at those things. Keep a good handle on your "gauges"—how you are doing physically, relationally, emotionally, spiritually, and so forth—and be intentional to get recharged so you don't burn out.

- Leaders take the initiative to **invest in people.** Love others around you really well. Be a catalyst in people's lives—help them see where they are succeeding and need growth. Give good feedback and also ask for feedback from others.

- Leaders **think like owners**. They have a high sense of responsibility and stewardship for what God has entrusted to them. When most people think, *Someone should do that,* leaders think, *I will figure out how we can do that.*

- A person can be either like a thermometer or a thermostat. Leaders **are thermostats**—they set the temperature, they don't just react to it.

- Leaders **call people to excellence**. They keep the vision in front of others. They **communicate loudly** (remove confusion) and **"lead with a limp"** (be open and authentic, not on a pedestal).

- Leaders **make it fun.** Serving together shouldn't be boring or drudgery—have a blast!

Looking for the Perfect Leaders?

This isn't about finding the perfect leaders for your ministry. There's only ever been one person who fit that description, and his job as the head of the church is not up for grabs. But it is about taking advantage of the incredible opportunity in front of you to find, develop, and deploy leaders in your ministry. As we'll see in the next couple chapters, these young men and women can't wait for you to call them to greatness and unleash them on mission. Are you ready?

CHAPTER 8

Call Them to Greatness

When I inherited the ministry of The Porch, we had about 100–150 people gathering each week. We met on the third floor of Watermark Church's office building in a room directly off the elevators. Most people just came for the message and to hang out afterward with their friends, but some of them—maybe a dozen or so—were volunteers who came a little early to help make the evening service run. When the volunteers showed up, we'd circle up real quick and figure out where everyone was going to be stationed for the evening. We'd say something like, "Hey, why don't you go greet people? You—how about you be an usher this week? And you—I like your T-shirt. Why don't you sit at the welcome center? You— stand by the elevators and say hi to people as they come in. And you—why don't you go into the parking lot and welcome people as they come in? OK, let's pray . . . ready, break!"

This worked, but barely. We struggled to find people who wanted to serve. There was lots of turnover with volunteers.

We weren't ever sure exactly who was going to show up each week or how long they would keep coming back. Many of the volunteers who did show up didn't seem all too excited to be there. And frankly, we were missing opportunities to engage attendees with the gospel.

Thank You, but Your Services Are No Longer Required

As I looked at the ministry, it became obvious to me what the problem was: our volunteers were uninspired. Why? Because there was no heroic vision. There was nothing that made serving at The Porch unique or even all that meaningful. We just needed warm bodies. I knew something had to change, so I sought the Lord, had a staff meeting, and then I did something kind of extreme—I fired all the volunteers.

I called all our volunteers together one week. I said, "Hey guys, who just wants to be a greeter? If you just want to be a greeter, you are respectfully relieved of your responsibilities. We're grateful for how you've served, but we no longer need people who simply greet. Who here just wants to be an usher? If so, this position is no longer available—we no longer have a need for people to just help visitors find their seats. Anybody just want to stand at the welcome desk? We're not looking for someone to just do this anymore. Thank you for your service, and we hope you keep coming, but not as a volunteer anymore. We no longer need you to just stand at the welcome desk. I'd encourage you to find another area of service at our church.

"*However*, if you want to be a missionary, if you want to be a pastor, a colaborer, if you want to be bivocational, if you want to give your life to this ministry, then come and die[1] with us! When you're helping people to their seats, if you think they might be feeling lonely, I want you to sit by them. When you meet someone, I want you to pastor them. If they tell you they are thinking about having an abortion, or they are struggling with suicidal thoughts, *you* are the pastor God has put in place. I need you to share the gospel every single week with every stranger you see in this place. I want you to be able to give your testimony in thirty seconds, three minutes, or thirty minutes, depending on how much time you have. I want you to memorize the Romans Road.[2] If you don't know how to share your faith, we will train you. We will disciple you. We will change the world together. Who's up for that?"

What's interesting is when we were just looking for greeters and ushers, we were practically begging people to come and serve. But when we put a heroic vision in front of people, and word got out that serving at The Porch meant something special, people started lining up to serve with us! Many of these were our old volunteers, but with a new mindset. They said things like, "You're going to disciple me? To call me to sobriety and purity, and actually hold me accountable to doing the things Scripture says? You're not going to water it down or dumb it down like everyone else is, and you're not going to beg me to come to your event? You're going to call me to something that matters? I am *so* in."

As my time at The Porch ended, we had more than two hundred volunteers serving weekly. They committed[3] to serving nearly fifty nights a year until late in the evening, even when they were tired after work. They committed to living above reproach in a pure and sober way, deeply connected with other Christians who held them accountable. They were all in with us on this mission! I don't say that to boast, but to show what God has done in and through his people as they caught the vision of what it means to serve and live on mission.

A Wicked Case of "Selfitis"

Nearly every young adult wants to be great. Like I mentioned in the introduction, 96 percent of Millennials think they will do something great in their lives. This can be a good thing—there's nothing inherently wrong with greatness. But there's a major obstacle to their achieving true greatness: an obsession with themselves.

Back in 2014, a website published an article claiming the American Psychiatric Association had designated "selfitis" as an officially classified mental disorder.[4] The article said the primary symptoms of this disorder were the obsessive taking and posting of selfies on social media. This rang true with readers and sounded like the young adults of our day, so it made a few headlines, and some major news outlets ran it as a story. There was only one problem: in small print toward the bottom of the page, the website disclosed it was part of a network of "the best news satire on the web." Whoops. Much like those people who think articles from the *Babylon Bee* or *The Onion* are the real deal, the public was duped. There's no such thing as "selfitis."

Or is there? Even though the original idea of selfitis was a hoax, it had enough of a ring of truth to it that some people started studying this concept. In late 2017, the *International*

Journal of Mental Health and Addiction (which is not, by the way, a satirical website) published an exploratory study of hundreds of young adults, reaching the conclusion that "selfitis" is, in fact, real and measurable.[5] To take it even further, the American Academy of Facial Plastic and Reconstructive Surgery recently reported 55 percent of plastic surgeons saw patients who specifically wanted to look better in selfies.[6]

As you minister to the next generation, you're trying to reach a generation obsessed with itself. Some of them quite literally have selfitis. They're getting surgery so they can look better on social media. Some of them are twenty-four-year-old adolescents, not even young adults.[7] The number one question they are asking when considering opportunities is, "What's in it for me?" They are coming to your church and asking, "What can the church do for me?" You've got to turn that on its head and say, "No, what can you do for the church? What can you do for God's mission?"

Jesus, We Want to Be Great

This self-obsession isn't a new problem. Even the church's first leaders were too focused on their own greatness as they got started. A couple thousand years ago, Jesus's disciples asked him the same kinds of questions: "Jesus, what can you do for us?" They were young adults who wanted to be great.

Here's just one example. Let me set the scene for you (Mark 10:32–45): Jesus and his disciples are heading to Jerusalem. He tells them when they arrive he's going to be delivered over to his enemies, condemned to death, handed over to the gentiles, mocked, spit on, flogged, and killed. Man, this must have seemed like a really good time for somber reflection and quietness of heart. But James and John decide *this* is the perfect moment to tell Jesus something that's really been on their minds lately. "Jesus, we're ready to die alongside you." Nope. "Jesus, we're ready to sacrifice anything for you and the mission." Not that either.

"Teacher . . . we want you to do us a favor. . . . When you sit on your glorious throne, we want to sit in places of honor next to you, one on your right and the other on your left" (vv. 35, 37 NLT). Yup. There it is. Jesus has just finished laying out for them how he's going to be tortured and killed, and all they can think about is what's in it for them. Sound familiar?

The topic of greatness was frequently on the disciples' minds. In fact, this was the number one thing they asked Jesus about and fought over. They asked who the greatest would be (Matt. 18:1). They argued with one another about who the greatest was (Mark 9:34; Luke 9:46). They disputed with each other about who would be regarded as the greatest (Luke 22:24). Greatness was their goal and their obsession.

On This Rock

And yet, these are the young adults whom Jesus used to accomplish his mission in the world. These are the young adults who affirmed Jesus was the Christ, the Son of the living God (Matt. 16:16). These are the young adults who received the keys to the kingdom of heaven (v. 19). These are the young adults whose faith would serve as the foundation the church was built on and whom the gates of hell would be powerless to stop (vv. 18–19).

These greatness-obsessed young adults are the same kinds of people Jesus wants to use today. He could have chosen anyone to change the world with, but he grabbed young adults and deployed them on mission. He took their desire to *be* great and redirected it to fulfill a Great Commission (28:18–20). He took their desire to be famous and shifted it to a desire to make him famous. He gave them a vision beyond themselves. That's what we must try to do with every young adult who serves with us and who hears our messages. We can dream big and pray big prayers, like "Lord, stretch out your hand and save every young adult in Dallas." We can consistently repeat our mission. For The Porch, it is "Surrendered to God, we are changing the world through the lives of young adults."

This is what you must do too. Not necessarily pray The Porch's specific prayer for your city or have the same specific mission statement, but give young adults a vision bigger than themselves. Don't bore them by playing church, pretending you have it all together. There's no place for pretending you're the perfect family. You have to come to young adults and tell them Christ has called them to something so much bigger than being stuck in their struggles and playing a game called church. He's called them to change the world! To go to the ends of the earth with his name. He's called them to live a life fully and radically devoted to him. There's no place for this "Sunday Christianity" we are so easily distracted by. That only leads to the weak vision and low commitment The Porch struggled with at first, and which you've very likely seen too.

But young adults will run through a wall if they have a heroic vision to follow.

Don't Ever Ask Anyone to Do Anything

You can't just ask young adults to live on mission or tell them they should be giving their lives away. It won't work. They'll eventually feel exploited, used, and discouraged. You have to *inspire* them to live out the mission God's called them to. This will take more work on your part. You aren't just handing out to-do lists; you're continually keeping a heroic vision in front of them. That might sound hard, but it's essential, because a weak vision (or a great vision never repeated and then forgotten) is the easiest way to discourage young adults from living out their great calling.

A few years ago I was cc'd on an email to a Porch volunteer. This email was to a girl who served in the ministry by leading the social media efforts. It was just one line, and it asked her to send out a particular tweet. Pretty short and sweet. And that was the problem. I followed up with my teammate who sent the email and said, "Don't ever just ask someone to do something. Never give them the 'what' without the 'why.' Tell her *why* it's important to send that tweet. Give her more color into what you're trying to do by putting the ministry in her hands. Remind her how that social media post fits into our vision of reaching young adults."

Never simply ask someone to do something. *We're not in the delegation business; we're in the inspiration business.*

I know this takes more work. But it also makes disciples. It allows young adults to understand the importance of what they're doing and how it directly fits into God's calling on their lives.

Are You Willing to Do What It Takes?

The Porch has several blog articles that communicate what it means to be truly great:

- "How to Be Great"[8]
- "How Will You Be Remembered?"[9]
- "The Greatest Sin"[10]
- "Revolutionary Humility"[11]

Some of you are probably rolling your eyes right now. You're thinking, *That sounds like a waste of time. I'm not up for all the vision stuff.* Well, then you're not up for reaching young adults. You might be content with having tasks delegated to you, but they are not. You need to adapt to incorporate what's effective in deploying them. At some point in the past, someone cared enough about your generation to begin investing in how to reach you. Now I'm just asking you to do the same. Are you willing?

CHAPTER 9

Give the Ministry Away

One conversation in Haiti changed the way I thought about evangelism. Back in 2012 I was part of a team that included about forty young adults on an international discipleship trip there. We spent the bulk of each day in villages our local mission partner was strategically trying to reach, walking from house to house sharing the gospel and giving out a few living essentials. Since no one on our team spoke Creole, all our conversations were through interpreters.

After a day of walking around the village of Minotree, our team debriefed on our struggles and successes. They were hot and tired, but on a high from having conversations with villagers about Jesus. People were getting saved and lives were being changed! But everyone had a common frustration—speaking through an interpreter. If you've done this before, you know how challenging it can be to communicate. You say a phrase, it's translated . . . they say a phrase, it's translated . . . you aren't sure who to look at . . . the conversation doesn't flow well, and it's easy to forget where you are in the dialogue.

My interpreter for the day was a young man from Minotree. He was also a Christian. As the team expressed frustration with the process of using an interpreter, I told them the genius solution I had used a few times. I just told my interpreter to share the gospel! He didn't need me to say anything. I'd stand quietly beside him, serving as the "excuse" for the conversation, while he shared the gospel and the conversation flowed freely.

My friend Ryan, a young adult in the business world, looked at me sort of confused and said, "You know it's his village, right?" Yes. Of course I did. That was the point. He could share the gospel in his language. "So, you're asking him to share the gospel door-to-door in his own village?" Exactly. I wanted him to share with his own people. He not only knew the language but also the culture, so we could just cut out the awkward and slow interpreting part. "So, you're wanting him to go door-to-door in his own community sharing the gospel?" At that point I thought, *OK, Ryan, you're being a slow learner and embarrassing yourself in front of your friends.* Then he said this: "But we don't do that."

Ryan was making the point that we don't go door-to-door in our communities sharing the gospel, so why should we ask this man to? He was right. It was convicting. Ryan then said, "We should do that. When I get back to Dallas, I'm going to do that."

And he did. He came back to Dallas and started something that became a movement called Unashamed.[1] After a few months of preparation and prayer, he asked people to join him for a two-day in-town mission trip. Seventy-two people showed up for it, which was interesting (see Luke 10:1). For some of them, they had only shared their faith for the first time two weeks before the trip. For all of them, it was a chance to engage their city with the gospel in a whole new way. Incredible stories came from that weekend:

- A Jewish gang leader who had just gotten out of prison trusted Christ.
- In South Dallas, several team members shared the gospel with one girl, who responded, "It is normally someone trying to turn a trick, or a drug dealer approaching me. This time it was you telling me God loves me. Your story has helped to set me free."
- One of the girls on the team said, "I was walking down the streets past the bars I used to bartend at. I know these streets, but this was the first time I was sharing my faith here."
- At ten o'clock on a Saturday night, when many of them used to be out getting drunk, hundreds of young adults gathered in our city-center park to worship God. One of them said, "We thought we were going to get kicked out of the park before it even started, since Bud Light was scheduled to have a massive scavenger hunt and promo party for Justin Timberlake. However, less than ten people showed up for that event, and they shut it down an hour early."

In the five years following that first Unashamed weekend trip, more than a thousand people have engaged our city with the gospel in a whole new way, and many people have trusted Christ or reconnected with his church body because of it. Unashamed weekends have become a monthly staple for The

Porch, and churches in other states have begun to use the Unashamed model to engage their own cities with the gospel.

Can I remind you that Ryan started this new ministry as a volunteer lay leader, not as a church staff member? Later on, well after the Haiti trip, we hired Ryan full-time to help us engage with our city, but he started and led Unashamed on his own time and dime while working a full-time business job. He was acting like a church staff member but was getting his paycheck from the corporate world. He didn't just come up with the idea for Unashamed, bring it to the church, and say, "Let the professional Christians figure out how to make this work." He thought like an owner and made it happen himself.

This wasn't unusual, which might surprise you—nearly every ministry at Watermark[2] was started the same way. Someone has an idea *and* they are willing to lead it, almost always as an unpaid volunteer. From a hiring standpoint, many of the new staff members brought on are people who were already doing the job part-time as a volunteer, and we simply started to pay them for doing it full-time.

Deploy, Don't Delegate

I didn't ask Ryan to start that ministry. I didn't convince him of the importance of reaching our city with the gospel and then provide him with a game plan to go execute. He had simply caught the vision of being called to greatness for the kingdom of God, saw a need to meet, and used his gifts to meet the need. It was a natural outcome of his being discipled in his faith, experiencing radical life change, and wanting others to experience the same thing.

Delegating tasks to young adults won't get you anywhere. What I'm talking about is different than delegating. You're not just telling them what to do but rather unleashing them under a heroic vision. Delegating tasks creates followers, but delegating authority creates leaders. You give them the vision, tell them what you hope to see God do in their midst, set big goals, and then tell them *they* are God's Plan A for making it happen.

If you haven't caught on yet, all I'm telling you to do is what Jesus did! He gave his disciples a heroic vision and told them nothing would stop them. In the Great Commission, Jesus gave his disciples some of his authority and then unleashed them. He told them to move throughout the world, teaching people the things he had taught them, baptizing them in the name of the Father, Son, and Holy Spirit. The last thing Jesus did before going up to heaven was to deploy his disciples. *He deployed young adults.* He gave them a heroic vision and then said, "Go and do it!" That's what we must do as well.

An Unusually Small Staff

The Porch has a relatively small staff for a ministry of its size. At its Dallas campus, when the ministry hit 3,500 weekly attendees there were only three people working full-time in the ministry: a director, a women's coordinator, and an administrative assistant. The reason this was possible, which might sound a little bit crazy, is due to the employment of so many volunteers to do the work of the ministry. This might be *the* "secret sauce" of The Porch.

The vast majority of people doing the real work of leading and ministering to young adults are volunteers who are themselves young adults: around two hundred volunteers are split into six teams, with twelve guys and girls coleading each of those teams. Each team has specific areas to focus on: parking cars, greeting at doors, giving high-fives, showing people to their seats, passing out information, welcoming new people, sitting with strangers, praying with people, sharing the gospel, offering biblical counsel, leading small groups, planning parties, taking pictures, designing graphics, creating videos, training other volunteers, and even helping prepare messages. But like we talked about earlier, none of these things are the main job of volunteers.

The number, structure, and job description of the teams aren't as important as the vision for what each volunteer is called to be: pastors to their peers, who are excellent hosts and expert evangelists. That is everyone's number one job description as a volunteer, and the rest is just details. No matter what someone's official volunteer job is, they should welcome people warmly and share the gospel clearly. People matter more than posts. Every time The Porch meets, each volunteer has one main job—to find "the one." And they aren't being told to look for their future spouse.[3] Their goal is to find at least one person they can connect with and have a meaningful conversation with about faith. It might mean engaging with a new person, encouraging a faithful attendee, or sharing the gospel with someone who is far from Christ. This means the ministry is asking for at least two hundred people each week to have an interaction with a volunteer who reminds them how much God loves them. More stories of life change come out of these conversations than from any I've had with people after teaching a message.

These volunteers invest a significant portion of the hours in their week serving young adults. And you know what? They love it! No one feels like they are getting exploited or ripped off or taken advantage of. Their volunteer surveys are full of testimonies about how serving is the best part of their week and the most fulfilling thing they are doing with their lives. They have been unapologetically asked to be an extension of the ministry staff without being on the payroll. They have been called to a bivocational life. Their leaders have asked them to dedicate multiple hours each and every week to doing the work of the ministry.

But they are also told (and shown) it won't just be work—they'll have a blast, laugh until they cry, and have a front-row seat to stories of God working that would seem impossible to believe if they hadn't witnessed them with their own eyes. Not everyone will sign up, but a lot of people do. Some Porch volunteers have even put serving in the ministry on their professional résumé. More and more, this means something to a potential employer. They know that person is committed and trained in service.

Ministry *through* People, Not *to* People

The principle that should underlie everything we do with volunteers is that it isn't our job as full-time church staff to do all the work of the ministry ourselves. This doesn't mean you and I kick up our heels and just collect a paycheck from people's tithes; it means we work hard to live as examples worth following (1 Cor. 11:1) and to equip other people to do the work of the ministry (Eph. 4:12) so the gospel can go forth in as many ways as possible. The work of Christian ministry shouldn't be done exclusively by those being paid to do it. I've heard it said the First Reformation in the church took God's Word from church leaders who were hoarding it and gave it back to the people; the reformation we need now is to take God's *work* from church leaders and give it back to the people.

For some of you, this will be hard. You're used to being the one in control, the one who's making all the decisions, and the main one whom people come to whenever they need some wise counsel. Why would you need to raise up other leaders, when God has put you there? Well, if you're not raising up the next generation of leaders, all you are is a bottleneck.

You can actually do more by doing less. By doing less of the direct work of the ministry yourself and focusing on empowering and building up others, you will expand the work of the kingdom many multiples beyond what you could do alone. You were made to multiply disciples, not your own personal influence. If you don't work through others, you might also be at risk for burnout, since you weren't made to handle it all on your own, and eventually your own resources will run out.

For others of you, it might be more of a question of not quite knowing how to do ministry *through* people instead of *to* people. Here are a few examples of what this can look like for us.

Don't Meet Alone

Not meeting alone isn't just a good idea for accountability purposes; it's an excellent way to make disciples. If I don't bring someone with me to a meeting, it's a wasted discipleship opportunity. If I'm meeting with anyone—whether it's a girl who's considering an abortion, a guy who is suicidal, or anyone dealing with a pastoral care issue—someone else is with me. The people I bring sometimes ask me if the other person will be comfortable with them coming. I tell them I won't be comfortable if they *don't* come. For the person we're meeting with, sometimes the question in their minds is one of confidentiality. "Sure, I can trust you as a pastor, but what about *that* guy/girl?" I explain to them that speaking in confidence literally means "with faith," and they can have faith we are both there to help them and will not gossip about their situation.

In that moment, the person coming with me is going to seminary! I don't mean that literally, but it's seminary-type training. (Or it should be, because you might not learn it there.) It's on-the-job training. And then the next time the same situation happens, I can say to the person who came with me the first time, "You go. And take someone with you."

The classic sequence goes something like this:

- I do it; you watch.
- We do it together.
- You do it; I watch.
- Now you go do it.

This doesn't add a complicated leadership development program to your plate; it adds a person to the meeting you'd be having anyway and allows them to learn from your example.

Help Them Discover Their Gifts

Before someone joins a Porch team as a volunteer, they go through a two-month training process called Roundabout.

Roundabout is offered four times a year to help connect new volunteers to Porch teams. This is one of the most strategic things the ministry can do, because it helps the teams—and the new volunteers—understand what the ministry is and where they best fit within it. The first few weeks of Roundabout give them an overview of the ministry's mission, vision, values, and culture. They're memorizing verses, learning how to communicate their testimony,[4] and gaining experience of engaging with "the one." Then the second half of Roundabout, called "shadowing," is when they get to experience what it's like to serve on the various teams. They rotate around to different teams each week, serving alongside each one, and by the end of the process they have a great idea of what each team does. And the leadership also has a great idea of which team(s) they would be a great fit for, which helps them make the right decision on where to deploy their new volunteers.

You might not need to implement an eight-week training process like this for your volunteers, but you must be intentional in helping them find and use their gifts.[5]

Empower Them to Lead

These leaders are unleashed by being empowered to act as an extension of the staff. They are not token leaders! They have responsibility for people (most Porch teams have thirty-plus members), money (tens of thousands of dollars in some cases), and messaging (some create videos and images seen by tens of thousands of people). Their leadership is absolutely essential to the success of the ministry. It quite literally would not happen without them.

The way The Porch unleashes its leaders is by empowering them with clear expectations and high trust. The team defines together what success looks like, provides what is needed to be successful, and watches people work. The clear expectations revolve around the "why" and the "what" of their responsibilities, and then they are trusted with the "how." It's important for both expectations and trust to exist together. If leaders are trusted but not given clarity, they could produce a lot of great effort that doesn't really fulfill the mission. And if there are clear expectations but no trust in the execution, this can produce hesitation and fear of doing the wrong thing.

If you're missing clear expectations and/or high trust, you won't be successful in unleashing your volunteers. But if you provide the right people with both of those things, you'll be blown away by what they can accomplish.

Hold Them Accountable

Trust is a two-way street. It's something given to leaders and volunteers, but it's also something they continually earn. They don't earn trust by performing successfully so much as they earn it by letting their leaders know when they *didn't*. This kind of transparency isn't just something that should be modeled as a staff; it's something that should be asked for and expected from those leading and serving in our ministry. This may range from "This event didn't go as well as it could have, and here's why . . ." to "I need to confess some sin to you."

We should have high standards for ourselves and for our leaders and volunteers, but we're not asking anyone for perfection. We're just asking for honesty, so we can work together to address whatever might be happening. Sometimes, but rarely, the result of this honesty can be asking someone to take a break from serving so they can focus on getting well. But most of the time the result will be a hug, a prayer, a plan of action and accountability, and gratitude for the privilege of serving our king together, marveling that he would use imperfect people like us to accomplish his perfect mission.

Give It to Live It

Giving ministry away might be one of the hardest things you'll ever do. After all, you may have gotten into ministry to do the exact thing I'm now telling you to hand off to someone else. You might have to redefine what it means for you to be "in ministry," from being the one who does it all to equipping others to do it all. But that's a biblical definition—one that will ultimately result in the body of Christ being built up (Eph. 4:12). Don't be ashamed to play the background and let others step up—for The Porch, that was how Unashamed was born. And it might just be how God does something great in your midst.

CHAPTER 10

Create Unique Shared Experiences

When I think about the times I've laughed the hardest in my life, the top five experiences would all be at Watermark staff functions. The most ordinary moments have become some of my most extraordinary memories as our senior pastor, Todd, made something otherwise normal into a game with a winner, a loser, and a consequence. We would "pastor hard" and play just as hard. Sure, sometimes there was a prize for winning, but I could guarantee there would always be a consequence for losing. I've had to take shots of Tabasco, swim in frozen ponds, take baths in eggnog, be covered in syrup and powdered sugar, and have some crazy impromptu haircuts.[1]

I know this might not sound like your kind of fun right now, but when you're with the right people and the stakes are high, it's always an amazing time. I've told Todd he's the best in the world at planning a party on a budget. It's safe to say I've laughed until I've cried *many* times on his staff. Some of the most unique experiences and unforgettable memories of my life have been with my fellow staff members, and many of them have become some of my closest friends.

A Carpool They'll Never Forget

Here's a recent example of how this looks for the Watermark team. At the beginning of every year, the entire staff goes on a three-day/two-night retreat to a camp outside of town. The main reason for this is to invest in relationships with each other and get a lot of "family time" away from the day-to-day distractions, commitments, and pressures of the job. But I'm not even talking about the retreat right now—I'm just talking about the drive out to the retreat. The location is about two hours away, and everyone is split into groups to carpool out there together. Mostly this time is full of good conversations and the occasional fun activity for the car to do together, which is great, but the last time I went, Todd kicked it up a notch. Before we left, everyone got this directive: "On your way out to the retreat, your car must shoot a thirty-second video of someone doing something crazy." That was it—no direction or limitations on what kind of thing it could or should be . . . just something crazy. And when we got to our retreat, we would watch all the videos together and vote on the top and bottom teams, with prizes and consequences, of course. Ready, break!

One team convinced a diamond store in the mall to loan them a ring, which they took and handed to a young man they'd never met before who was willing to propose to a girl he'd never met before. (He was in on the joke, but she understandably replied, "No way—I don't even know you!" to his impassioned proposal.[2]) Another team had a couple guys put on a chicken costume and a hot dog suit to protest at a meat store, only to be chased out by a knife-wielding cashier.[3] In an awkwardly humorous video, one gal went around to people's tables at a Starbucks and tasted their drinks without their permission.[4] One guy shaved his head and beard completely down-to-the-skin bald. One girl rode through a car wash . . . on the hood of the car! And the winner? Well, he got his belly button pierced on camera. Now *that's* commitment!

Hear me on this: I'm not telling you to steal someone's coffee or get your belly button pierced. But I am telling you one simple thing transformed an otherwise monotonous two-hour drive into an unforgettable opportunity for team building, memory making, and fun. The anticipation to watch everyone's videos was palpable. The reactions were hilarious. And the people who carpooled were bonded together in a way that would have never happened otherwise. Their unique shared experience brought them closer together than any conversation could have.

"Pics or It Didn't Happen"

The point of the road trip videos wasn't to create a "social media moment" the staff could share on their profiles for some likes or to show people how fun they are. In fact, Watermark generally asks staff to keep things like this "in the family" and not share them publicly. For one, what church wants to be known as the Starbucks bandits? There is also no desire to contribute to any stereotype that "the only thing church staffers do is play around and grab coffee." Like I said, we would "pastor hard," and that is serious work. We definitely put our time in. Things like this are also kept offline because it's way too easy for living life together to become secondary to *showcasing* it. If documenting these unique experiences becomes just as important as actually having them, we've got a problem. Some of my best memories have no photographic evidence whatsoever.

But above all, the point of the road trip task, and other unique shared experiences like it, is to connect people and build strong teams.

The Power of Teams

Having people work and serve on healthy teams is important for a lot of reasons. First, healthy teams make disciples. Discipleship is all about doing life together, seeing someone do something, then learning from them how to do it. Being on a team together is a great way for people to learn from each other. Second, healthy teams build ownership. As people work together toward a common goal, they feel a high level of personal responsibility to accomplish the team's objectives, especially when they can see exactly how they fit into the team's vision and objectives. Third, healthy teams help more work get done. The more people you have working together, the more they can accomplish. And fourth, healthy teams make things more fun! Any introverts out there might not always agree with me, but working with other people on something brings more fun, laughter, and joy than you would experience just on your own.

The Problem with Teams

Now, I've mentioned "healthy teams" quite a bit, but a big problem with a lot of teams is people don't enjoy being on them because the teams aren't healthy. The members don't really know or trust each other. A team without trust isn't really a team; it's just a group of individuals working together, often making disappointing progress. We all remember those group projects in school—was there anyone who honestly looked forward to them? Maybe the slackers did, knowing the type-A students would drag them along for the ride so as to not risk their own grade. But for those who just wanted to get their work done, being on a team felt like a dramatic and unnecessary obstacle to achieving their own personal performance.

Out in the business world, plenty of people dislike teamwork too. In the corporate world, I watched as a team was torn apart and people lost their jobs simply because two members couldn't get along. Nearly two-thirds of employees sometimes or always work in teams, and it isn't always pretty. Almost half of those people feel friction working with colleagues, and one-third have thought about looking for new work because of the challenge of working with others.[5]

How does this look in your ministry? Do you struggle to get enough people on your teams? Do a few people perform most of the work while everyone else watches? Do your teams effectively know and use everyone's gifts? Do teammates trust one another? Does managing the health of your teams take more work than it's worth? Do people actually *enjoy* being on teams with one another? I've talked with enough pastors to know church teams can be some of the most dysfunctional out there.

What Makes a Great Team?

You don't have to look hard to find the reason for problems on a dysfunctional team—it's generally the people. You also don't have to look too hard to find the reason for great performance on a healthy team—again, it's the people! Team members can be the source of both dysfunction and health on a team. The question is why, and what can we do about it?

If you want to find out what makes a great team, you can do what most people do with just about every other question we have . . . ask Google. But I don't mean type a question into the Google search bar, which happens about forty thousand times every second.[6] I mean we can literally learn what Google as a trailblazing, innovative company figured out about healthy teams. A few years ago, Google launched a project to figure out what made the perfect team.[7] Now, a cutting-edge tech giant is not a ministry, but I think we can learn something from them.

Here was Google's number one takeaway about healthy teams: specific personality types, skills, or backgrounds didn't make any difference. What distinguished the good teams from the dysfunctional ones was *how teammates treated one another.* The best teams weren't just focused on efficiency or production; they were places where people didn't have to put on a "work face" at the office, were socially sensitive to one another, had above-average levels of emotional intelligence, weren't afraid to take risks, were all able to contribute, and felt confident and safe they wouldn't be embarrassed, punished, or rejected for speaking up.

I don't know about you, but this is encouraging to me. It means we all already have *exactly what we need* to have incredible teams in our ministries. We don't need a bunch of specialized degrees or a particular blend of personalities or, frankly, even this book—we just need healthy people. It's way more about the "how" of teams working together than the "who" of their members. But Google didn't have to tell us this; God already did. Healthy teams are full of people who are directed by the Holy Spirit (Eph. 5:18) and who "Do to others as you would have them do to you" (Luke 6:31). Healthy teams bear one another's burdens, encourage one another, accept one another, are kind to one another, tolerate one another, forgive one another, and generally practice the "one another" commands of Scripture.[8] This doesn't mean all teams of Christians will automatically be healthy. But it absolutely means any team of Christians can be an incredible team. There is hope for your teams, no matter how healthy or unhealthy they might be right now.

Seven Principles for Team Building

So, how can we, as leaders, build healthy teams? I got to learn these principles from my friend Kyle, who is probably the best team builder I know. He's led a ton of healthy and productive teams over the years, and he shared how he's been able to do it in a talk at Watermark's 2018 Church Leaders Conference.[9] Here are the highlights:

1. **Be courageous.** You must be rooted in Scripture, unafraid to take a stand, and willing to do whatever God calls you to do.
2. **Bring energy.** No matter your wiring, you want to be excited about what you're doing and pass that excitement and energy on to others.

3. **Have fun.** Life is too short to not do ministry with those you love. Invest in your relationships with each other. One of the best ways to love each other more is to have fun together!

4. **Know yourself.** Pay attention to your own heart and walk with Christ. Know what your gifts and weaknesses are, and build a team around them.

5. **Play chess, not checkers.** In checkers, all the pieces do the same thing. In chess, each piece has a specific ability and purpose. Learn your team's gifts so you can use them in the best way.

6. **Set the bar.** Set clear expectations, direction, and vision. Then get out of the way! Build trust with one another, and then give people responsibility, decision-making authority, and accountability.

7. **Provide candid feedback.** Tell people what they need to hear, even the hard things. Handle conflict biblically. Admonish and encourage as needed.

There's some serious gold here! Each of these points could be at least a chapter on its own, but I'd like to focus on #3 and unpack a little more about building relationships with each other and having fun together.

The Power of Shared Experiences

If you're like me, you read a list like the one Kyle developed and you think, *Team building sounds like it takes a lot of work.* It does. But team building also takes a lot of *fun.* You might call it "the serious business of having fun together." I fully believe teams that pray and play together can change the world together. You can't build a ministry team if the only time you spend together is while you're "in the foxhole" doing the ministry. Teams work much better together when their members have strong friendships and high levels of trust with one another, and one major way these develop is from sharing experiences and having fun together. Shared experiences have the ability to fuse people together, often even those who wouldn't have made sense together outside of that context. I've seen it happen time after time.

Now, when I say "fun," you don't have to envision some hokey icebreaker game wedged in at the start of a meeting. You also don't have to picture some hypercompetitive activity ending with a few people dominating and everyone else just wishing it were over. There isn't some magical activity that works to bond every team, and there's a reason plenty of people just want to roll their eyes the second you start talking about "team building." It's often awkward and lame because it feels forced.

You need to find something you can do together as a team with the right balance of stress and meaning. Doing things together is important, because research has shown the impact of positive experiences is amplified when they are shared with other people.[10] Research has also shown the greater the stress and meaning a team activity has, the more powerful a bonding experience it is.[11] That's one reason why Navy SEALs who go through BUD/S training together are family for life—the experience they shared was one of the most stressful and meaningful our country has to offer.

The most memorable team building experiences don't feel like a normal day at the office; they are unique and slightly outside of people's comfort zones. Perhaps they build in a little tension by having friendly consequences for losing, like the eggnog bath I mentioned at the beginning of the chapter. We can build in meaning by reminding people of the importance of investing in time together, but we should also try to add meaningful elements to the fun. For example, during the road trip video challenge, everyone was also encouraged to look for opportunities to share the gospel as a team. It doesn't get much more meaningful than that!

Shared experiences are the gift that keeps on giving for your teams, because recalling the experience sparks even greater bonding, especially when there is a meaningful narrative about it.[12] That might sound a little stuffy, but all it means is that conversations including things like "Oh, man, do you remember when we . . ." reinforce friendships, which is something we've probably all experienced. When you make a memory together and then talk about it later, you grow even closer to the people you share the memory with.

The Magic of a Retreat

A retreat is one of the best things you can do to encourage bonding on your team, and these can be prioritized on a lot of levels. For example, once a year the entire Watermark staff gets away together for a few days. In the spring and fall, The Porch staff team takes a weekend retreat with its core volunteer leaders. And then each of those volunteer leaders also takes their Porch team on retreats in the spring and fall. It can seem like a lot of work, but it is effective.

A few years ago, I was part of a retreat to a lake house in East Texas with about twelve other leaders to plan another year of ministry. While we were driving out there, I saw a sign saying there was a flea market in town that weekend. I got an idea for making a memory: everyone gets $20 to spend at the flea market, and whoever can negotiate the best prize wins. Whoever gets the worst prize . . . well, you're swimming in the lake at midnight. And off we went!

The flea market in this small East Texas town was a blast. It was the best people-watching experience of my life! We saw a man with a pet chicken, and the official dress code of this event must have been overalls with no shirt. I thought this would be the unique experience we'd all share together . . . but that was before I saw a guy standing next to his race car. He was handing out free tickets to a race that night. So, of course, we grabbed some tickets and directions to the race, and went back to the house to get ready.

As we piled into our cars and began to drive the back roads of East Texas out to the track, we all wondered what the race would be like. We drove for what felt like forever on a single-lane road with trees completely hanging over us on either side, with no signs of a racetrack. We kept going, turning at stop signs in the middle of nowhere, until we hadn't seen another car for about forty-five minutes. And then on the horizon there was a glow. As we drove closer, we could see the glow was coming from stadium lights. It was the racetrack. With people at it. In the middle of *nowhere*.

We pulled up and used our tickets to get in. And, no lie, they literally announced we were there. "Please welcome the young adults group from Watermark Church!" The cars roared around a dirt track. There were wrecks and winners. There were checkered flags and Cheetos. We were having the time of our lives. They gave us tickets to "the pit," and we got to go where all the race car drivers were with their cars. Dust was flying everywhere, so we affectionately called the place the "dust bowl."

A day at a flea market turned into a memorable evening at a racetrack. People still tell this story in the ministry—it's been passed down from team to team. We made a memory together, and it has become legendary.

These retreats don't have to be extravagant experiences. They can be something in town and low budget. The key is to take the time to do them and to invest the time into making them creative and meaningful.

Living on Mission Together

It doesn't get any more meaningful than living on mission together. Whether it's at a weekend Unashamed trip like I mentioned in the last chapter or overseas on an international discipleship trip, both are examples of incredibly powerful ways to bond teams together. I remember being on mission in Brazil, taking a six-day trip down the Amazon to share the gospel with people in villages along the way. We lived on a metal boat and slept in hammocks. We went hunting for alligators. We heard jaguars roar in a way that would make the hair on the back of your neck stand up. We played soccer with kids. And we shared the gospel and got to watch Jesus save people. It forged deep bonds of friendship, and we still talk about those trips.

I have to think this is what it was like for Jesus and his disciples too. They constantly went places together, ate together, and got to share powerful and unique experiences with one another. I imagine they spent many an evening around the campfire talking about the incredible things they witnessed and got a chance to participate in that day. "Can you believe how Jesus told the wind and waves to be still?" "Man, do you remember how Jesus told Lazarus to come out of the grave . . . and he did?" "Did you see the demon come out of the other guy?" "How many baskets of bread and fish did *you* have left over?" They had to have been an incredibly close team.

Investing in Team Building

Some of the best shared experiences I've had have been completely unplanned, but most involved some amount of planning and investment. Sometimes it's an investment of resources; it's always an investment of time and energy. Both are important, and both can be challenging to do.

Experiences don't have to be expensive to be memorable and powerful. Those tickets to the unforgettable race were completely free. But our team and staff budgets have line items for every retreat we do, because we know it generally takes some money to pull them off. Dedicating money toward team building will help make sure it happens.

More importantly, in order to make retreats and other team building events happen, we all have to clear our calendars and prioritize time together. This is something you'll have to fight for and be intentional about, because it gets harder to do the larger your teams are and the busier you are. One of your jobs as a leader is to be intentional in investing the time and resources it will take to build your teams. I believe it's one of the most important investments you can make in your ministry.

Farkle: Fun and Free!

One of the best things I have done as staff and with teams just happens to be completely free, completely flexible, and limited only by your own creativity. I'm talking about Farkle. A quick online search will give you the basics of the game: all you need are some dice, a way to keep score, and willing participants. The way I have played, it doesn't matter who wins; it only matters who has the lowest score after the last round, because they are the loser who has to do whatever consequence the team comes up with before the game starts. This creates an intense desire to not be the loser, which adds to the stress and meaningfulness of the game (bonding!) and also creates hilarious shared memories as everyone watches the loser perform whatever the consequence is (more bonding!).

Here's how Farkle took one staff meeting from normal to unforgettable. My story might make you a bit squeamish, but I promise there's a point to it all. A girl had lost a game of Farkle the week before, and the consequence the players had come up with was to chew and blow a bubble with a wad of bubble gum . . . made from pieces of gum thirty other people at the staff meeting had already chewed. Gross! This gal lost well, and she faithfully gathered the gloppy pieces of gum straight from people's mouths into a Styrofoam cup, wadded them together, and blew a bubble in front of everyone, to big applause. Major props to her.

But then things got a little more interesting.

Someone threw out the idea of pitching in some money to see who else would now be willing to take the pre-pre-chewed gum wad and blow another bubble with it. One guy raised his hand and said he'd be willing to do it for $50. Another offered to do it for $40. This went on until one guy said he'd do it for $10. That might sound crazy to you, but this guy used to ride rodeo bulls, so chewing used gum probably felt pretty tame to him. He earned his $10 with a great bubble. But then things got *even more* interesting.

While this guy was chewing and blowing the bubble, another gal, Jane, was sitting close to him and barely containing her gag reflex as she watched. She looked miserable, and she wasn't even the one doing it. So, of course, when he was done with the gum, I asked her, "Jane, how much for you to do it?!" The entire staff immediately started cheering and chanting for Jane to chew the pre-pre-pre-chewed wad. When we quieted down, you could see the wheels turning in her head. Could any amount of money possibly be worth it?

Everyone's got a price—hers was $500. I talked her down to $100. Jane grabbed the gum and the hundred bucks, choked back her gag reflex a few times, and brought the house down by chewing the gum and blowing a great bubble. She became an instant legend, and our entire staff got an incredibly fun shared memory, all from some dice and a few pieces of gum.

Powerful and fun shared experiences can come when you least expect them. But even more importantly, these experiences happen when you, your leadership, and your teams are committed to allowing them to happen. They happen when your people understand the importance of having a culture valuing fun, relationship building, and memory making. Jane had been around Watermark for a long time, and she knew fun was important and sometimes involved doing uncomfortable things. Even beyond making a quick few bucks, she did it because she understood the value of playing together and making a memory.

This Works, but Find What Works for You

On your teams, you probably don't want to begin with the pre-pre-pre-chewed gum Farkle loss.[13] I can pretty much promise it won't go over well. But choose what works for you, and I think you'll be surprised and encouraged by how much of a difference it makes in the health of your teams as you prioritize creating unique shared experiences for your staff and volunteers.

CHAPTER 11

Remember the Vision

I believe one conversation can change someone's entire life. This happened to my friend Hank—and here's how it happened, in his own words:

> I was an insecure twenty-seven-year-old, four months into my dream job when I had an unlikely encounter with someone who offered me a conversation I deeply desired. He asked me about me, and about me again, and about me some more—followed by something about a scale from 1–10 and where I might go when I die. After all this, he told me to let him know if I ever made it to this thing called The Porch.
>
> *Yeah, ok . . . sure*, I thought. *One day . . . maybe.* A few months later, after getting invited to The Porch by a random pregnant woman at a restaurant, I decided I couldn't avoid it any longer. I would have to go see what was to be seen at this "big deal" Porch thing. I made arrangements to go the following Tuesday.
>
> Determined to avoid awkward small talk, I agreed to meet a friend beforehand—who was late. I was shyer and more

withdrawn than I should have been. I wasn't confident enough to meet new people. I just tried to blend in with my surroundings. My phone became really interesting. As did the line to get coffee—which I wish had been longer, because soon I was standing alone, coffee in hand, hoping no one would notice my presence. Unfortunately for me, a tall curly haired guy noticed my existence and made a beeline toward me. In my head, I wondered what I could possibly say to downplay my obvious seclusion.

"Traffic was pretty terrible, huh?" His first five words to me began a friendship that would start me on a long journey of healing. That volunteer was the first of a long line of Porch volunteers who, in so many ways, are responsible for sharing God's joy with me, forever changing my life's journey.

If I had to list the most significant influencers in my twenty-nine years of life, The Porch—and its volunteers—would be near the top of the list. Every Tuesday they made me feel as if I were the center of the universe. They opened their lives to me in conversation, sharing their trials and triumphs. They spent time with me outside of The Porch, showing me what manhood means: responsibility, leadership, respect for women, submission to God. They talked with me. They asked me about life, about work and girls and friends, about family and hurts and healing. They taught me how to read Scripture. They drew me out of the shell that had started to become my home.

And at the end of the day, I am told their heads hit their pillows and they thanked God for me. They thanked him for the privilege to serve and love someone like me. And prayed I would know him more. I very much needed to know I mattered, that I counted because of Christ. They made sure I knew it.

After being around these volunteers for just a few weeks, I knew joining them was my destiny. The people who wore The Porch shirt embodied everything I saw Christ calling me to be. And on a cold Tuesday evening in December 2014, I donned that hallowed shirt for the first time. I looked in the mirror and "The Porch" stared proudly back at me. No, it wasn't a uniform. To me, this was a legacy. I had joined the long list of those before me who had reached out to thousands of young adults like me and altered their lives.

Of all I've been privileged to do over the years, wearing that volunteer shirt has been one of the highest honors. Putting it on still feels like putting on armor or football pads. There is an enchantment to it. It symbolizes perseverance under trial, dying to self, integrity in life, grace under pressure, faithfulness to Christ, and, for so many lost young adults in Dallas, hope to a hurting world.

If you're volunteering at The Porch, you're not just joining a team; you're joining a legacy. You have an important chapter to write in God's story of The Porch, a story that started before you and will continue after you leave. This is your chapter. You have partnered with God to share his love with a simple yet profound message: "You matter. You matter more than the world."

People are coming to The Porch from every corner of the city. They're coming in nursing scrubs, high heels, and workout clothes. They're coming with worked shifts and tired faces and new jobs and individuality and all the expectation that comes with being a twenty- or thirtysomething. They come with broken homes, broken lives, crushed spirits, stolen innocence, and a desire to mask it all. But God is always up to the challenge, no matter how difficult the task. And he always brings the right people to do the job that needs to get done.

For you Porch volunteers, this is your year, your Tuesday—
your chance to give someone else the hope Christ offers—the
kind of hope that comes wrapped in a smile and a T-shirt saying, "The Porch."

As you've read, Hank did go on to become a Porch volunteer
after his life was so profoundly impacted by one. After he'd
served with us for a while, he wrote those words in a letter to
the new volunteers who were joining his team to give them a
sense of how incredibly important their roles were in finding
and engaging with "the one." I can't think of an example that
better captures the feeling so many Porch attendees have the
first time they come, as well as the impact volunteers can have
on them. Like I said earlier, I honestly believe more life change
comes out of the conversations people have with volunteers
after the message than from what people hear during the message. God works powerfully through his people!

We ended up including Hank's letter in the training packet
given to every single new Porch volunteer. It reminded us all of
why we do what we do—it isn't to build a large, world-changing
ministry; it's to have world-changing conversations one person
at a time. It's a great example of our ministry vision being played
out in real life.

From the Front Porch to the Back Patio

I haven't yet explained to you why The Porch is called what it is.
The way Hank felt when he first showed up on a Tuesday night
is an accurate description of what's happened to so many young
adults today, and is exactly why we chose our name.

Let's take it back to 1975 for a minute, before I was even born. There was an essay written that year titled "From Porch to Patio"[1] describing a cultural shift in people that led to an architectural shift in houses. Back in the day, people used to live out in the open on their front porches, sharing life and building community with their neighbors through impromptu life-on-life interactions as well as lengthier conversations. Young men and women courted one another on porches, and many an engagement proposal happened on one. People could look out on the world from their front porches and see whom they could help, whether a stranger passing by or a neighbor working on their home or vehicle. From their porches, people would welcome guests into the comfort and community of their homes. A front porch was a place of authenticity, connection, and happiness.

But then, as culture changed and the pace of modern existence accelerated, the life that used to be lived in public on front porches shifted away to the isolated oases of back patios. With ever-more-packed calendars, people drove straight into their attached garages and detached from their neighbors. They didn't come out of the privacy of their homes to do anything except drive somewhere else. The other people living on their street became strangers, and communities became more disconnected. The porch-centered life largely became a relic of a bygone era, and front porches shrank as privacy-fenced back patios took over.

If things were like that more than forty years ago, imagine what it's like today. The trends of disconnection and withdrawal the essay described haven't reversed themselves; they've only accelerated. Today's young adults in America are the most likely generation to suffer from loneliness.[2] The majority of young adults don't know their neighbors' names.[3] They're disconnected from one another and from what matters most. They are busy and bored, moving aimlessly from one thing to the next. Desperate to be loved, they're looking for satisfaction and hope in all the wrong places, turning to serial relationships and the privacy of their own addictions and anxieties instead of connecting deeply with others and sharing their burdens openly. They do this all while putting on the same mask of false happiness—both online and offline—that has made suburbia notorious. Today's "back patio" can be a dark place, whether it's a physical escape or a digital one.

It's why The Porch exists, a ministry with a vision to point the current and future generations of young adults back to what they so desperately need—a deep relationship with Jesus and authentic relationships with one another. The want is to bring back the kind of life that was lived on front porches, and that is also the reason behind the lantern in the middle of the logo: we're the light of the world, here to blast away at the darkness in peoples' lives in a way that cannot be hidden or ignored (Matt. 5:14–16).

And our city desperately needs this. If you're not from around here, you might think of Dallas as being the "buckle of the Bible belt"—surely things can't be that bad, right? After all, our metro area has the highest percentage of people claiming to be Christians of anywhere in the country.[4] Well, we're also not just listed as a surprisingly dangerous city from a crime standpoint;[5] we're nearly tops in the country at being vain, jealous, and lustful, out-sinning even notorious New Orleans.[6] Trust me when I say the young adults of Dallas need Jesus.

Wherever you are, your city or town has darkness and needs Jesus too. You're the light of the world if you're working to reach young adults with the hope of the gospel. It doesn't matter what your ministry's named, what resources are at your disposal, or if you're even an "official" ministry, as long as your mission and Master are the same.

What We're on Mission to Do

I briefly mentioned the mission of The Porch in an earlier chapter: "Surrendered to God, we are changing the world through the lives of young adults." A few years ago, we made a small change to this statement that made a huge difference. It used to read, "Surrendered to God, we will change the world through the lives of young adults." It had been that way for years, but a volunteer Porch leader said to me one day, "Why does it say 'we *will* change the world' in our mission statement? I see world-changing things happening all around us *right now!*" So we took her advice and changed our mission to "we *are* changing the world." It was a subtle but important shift, making our mission something present and tangible instead of just aspirational and future-oriented. We're not putting off change until tomorrow; we're pushing for it today.

A Leaky Vision

Here's the problem, though—vision leaks. And by "leaks" I don't mean it flows out of me and soaks deeply into the sponge of everyone's hearts and minds so they think about it all the time. No, I mean exactly the opposite: vision leaks, as in it leaks out and is forgotten, like it's been poured into a sieve. My capacity to hold on to and live out a vision isn't watertight. No one's is—this leakiness affects me, you, and certainly those working and volunteering in our ministries. When we lack this vision, this clarity and excitement about what God has us on earth to do, the natural result is ineffective ministry. Having discouraged volunteers is the easiest and fastest way to kill a ministry, and having a weak, forgotten vision is the easiest way to discourage volunteers.

Plugging My Own Leaks

And let's face it: ministry can be really hard and discouraging. It easily becomes hazardous to my soul if I let it act as a substitute for my own dynamic relationship with Jesus. It can trick me into feeling like I'm always doing Jesus-y things even when I'm not, or that my motives are pure when they're often murky. It's too easy to drink my own Kool-Aid and believe my own press by letting what others think about my walk with Christ become what I actually believe about myself. Most people only see me onstage; they don't see what it takes for me to be up there and not be a hypocrite doing it.

In reality, I'm like a flower in a vase: I might look good for a while on my own, but I'm dying unless I'm continually being refreshed and refilled by the Vine (John 15:5). There's no way I can inspire others with a compelling vision unless my own tank is full.

And how do I fill my tank? By filling the bath.

That's right. I love baths and take them often. Don't think about that too long. But nothing is more relaxing and refreshing to me than filling the tub in my house with steaming hot water, lighting up a candle or two, dialing up some music, and reflecting on God's truth. It's like a free mini-vacation any night of the week. I'm encouraged and inspired as I soak. I even wrote part of this book from the bathtub.

Your thing might not be taking baths, but you need to know what fills your tank and renews your vision. You need to regularly refill or you'll become a casualty of the ministry cause, and you won't be able to live out or pass on any kind of healthy vision at all.

The "5 Cs" of Vision-Casting

At The Porch, I witnessed a lot of talk about casting vision in a way that people can "get it." There are certainly a lot of different ways to go about this, but during my time there we came up with a few pointers I have found to be helpful for use as a staff, and also as passed on to volunteer leaders to incorporate into their own vision-casting with their teams. Let's call them the "5 Cs."

1. Cast vision **convincingly**. This goes back to the bathtub. I have to be refreshed myself before I can refresh others, and personally convinced of the vision in order to convince anyone else. If I'm not all-in on the vision, people will see through the sham right away. Don't be afraid to put some emotion and effort into it too.

2. Cast vision **constantly.** I can't just say the vision once and expect people to get it. People have to be reminded of the vision all the time—it leaks, remember? Someone once told me I can know I've said something enough when people begin to make fun of me for it.

3. **Celebrate** the vision being lived out. What's celebrated gets replicated. Frequently telling stories of people living out the vision and of people whose lives were impacted by the vision keeps everyone's tanks brimming with gratitude and amazement for what God is doing.

4. **Communicate** the vision in your own voice. We all have different styles. One isn't necessarily better than another. What matters is if it's authentic and real. I try not to compare my vision-casting style with others, and I encourage others not to compare theirs with mine. We can definitely learn from each other, but we don't have to mimic one another.

5. **Call** people to something heroic. Go back to the first couple pages of chapter 8 for an example of this. A vision just for parking cars isn't going to inspire or motivate anyone. But a vision for being a pastor who happens to be serving in the parking lot just might. We want to call people to greatness.

Remember What's at Stake

It's so easy to forget what's really at stake here. Impacting young adults isn't just an abstract concept about having a more effective ministry; souls and eternal destinations are literally hanging in the balance. The average life expectancy in the States is around seventy-nine years, so it can feel like we have a lot of time to reach young adults. But no one knows when their life will end, and the time to be sure about eternity is *now*. Nothing else matters. This gospel-driven urgency is the engine behind a compelling and heroic ministry vision. Without it, everything else is just noise and empty movement.

I learned this lesson shortly after I started in full-time ministry. When I became a pastor, one of my first responsibilities was to help with a funeral. A very wealthy man had died and left his wealth to his two sons. Since his sons were in their twenties, and I was the young adults' pastor, I was asked to go with our senior pastor to visit the family.

We drove up to their pristine house on a gated estate. When we walked inside, I had never seen anything like it. The hallways were big. The furniture was big. The paintings were big. Everything was huge! But something inside looked a little funny— there were these little notes stuck all over the walls. I asked the young men what those were about, and they said that in their dad's final days, he had wanted to be surrounded by God's Word, so every note had a Scripture verse on it. Facing his own mortality, their dad had soaked himself in Scripture and shared the gospel with anyone and everyone he could.

I asked if there was anything else they'd like to say about their dad. The two sons looked at each other and said in unison, "He said: 'Don't wait.'" They explained that, as death crept up on their father, he would cry out, "Don't wait! Don't wait like I did! Go and tell them about Jesus! Live for Jesus!"

That's the advice I'd pass on to you—don't wait! Share the gospel and reach young adults with the extreme urgency of a dying man. Life and death are hanging in the balance.

Remember What's Possible

Part of remembering and rekindling the vision for your ministry is recalling what's possible. We can all give the Sunday school answer that all things are possible with God (Matt. 19:26), but sometimes on a practical level what we do in ministry can feel like a lost cause. "Is God *really* going to use me to reach the next generation? Am I laboring in vain, or is this accomplishing something?" As I look at the sheer lostness of many young adults around me, or think about the hundreds of thousands of young adults in my city who don't know Jesus, or the millions more in our country and around the world in the same situation, I can get discouraged. The hill just seems too big and steep to climb. But then I recall what God has done, and it gives me hope.

I remember seeing a book called *PostSecret*, where people would confess their biggest secrets on a postcard and mail them to the author to be published. I guess there is something liberating about sharing the often ugly truth about yourself. But there's also power in putting a different kind of truth out there.

A few years ago, we ran an experiment at The Porch in which we asked people to share their testimonies and post them on Twitter with the hashtag #MyStory. On Tuesday evening at seven o'clock, before we met, there was not a single #MyStory on Twitter. But I woke up Wednesday to more than 4,500 of them. These were powerful stories:

Josh J.D. & a bottle of pills. Thought ending my life was better than to live. But Christ saved me from the bottle & filled it with GRACE! #mystory

Miranda THEN: Suicidal, bipolar, adulteress, sexually molested as a child. NOW: full of life, pure, holy, redeemed, beautiful, strong. #mystory

Ryan Weak, insecure, a coward for Christ, & hiding behind a wall of pride. Forgiven & set free by his unexplainable love! #mystory

Angela Porn addict, value defined by men, self-destructive. Set free from guilt and shame by the power of my risen Lord. I am redeemed! #mystory

Liz Tired of being the good girl so I explored all the world offers. Dying in guilt and shame, I ran to a Redeemer who calls me clean. #mystory

Dan Over-churched self-righteous atheist with father issues. Rescued and redeemed by a Holy Father. Now I'm unashamed of the Gospel. #mystory

Bryan Porn, sex addicted, drug pusher, full of pride and anger. Believed a true story about Jesus. Forever changed by Him and for Him. #mystory

Wade I was drowning in depression & self-hate as years of drunkenness, porn, sex, selfishness enslaved me. By grace, Christ set me free. #mystory

Kelsey Jesus replaced my depression with joy, my insecurity with knowing I am loved by God, & my shame with forgiveness & redemption! #mystory

Corey Alone inside and outside my mind, desperate for someone to love me. Addicted to porn, smoke, drugs, alcohol. God saved my soul. #mystory

There are literally *thousands* more of these testimonies of freedom. Stories of life change like these are the lifeblood of ministry. There's power in sharing them. They fill our tanks, renew our vision, remind us God is in the business of changing lives, and give us confidence our labor for him is never in vain (1 Cor. 15:58).

Why Not You?

You might not witness thousands of stories like these. You might only witness a few, or maybe even none—at least not in a way you'll know about on this side of eternity. But it will be worth it. Be faithful every day, share those stories on repeat, and remind people of the heroic vision and mission they are living out. If you aren't seeing the stories yet, celebrate the faithfulness of those who are pouring themselves out for the gospel with no apparent fruit to show for it. With God, no one is a lost cause, and *all* things really are possible. God is going to do something great for his name's sake. Why not with us? Why not with you?

Conclusion

Starting a Revolution

I've spent a lot of time thinking about revolutions. I don't know if you've realized this, but every revolution has had young adults at its epicenter. History has plenty of examples of this. In the French Revolution, Napoleon was twenty-six when he became a military commander.[1] In the American Revolution, more than a dozen signers of the Declaration of Independence were thirty-five or younger.[2] In the Sexual Revolution, Hugh Hefner was twenty-seven when he founded *Playboy*.[3] I could keep going. At the heart of all those movements were young adults. Today, those revolutionaries would all have been Millennials.

I want to be part of a revolution that covers the world with the gospel! I believe you do too. If we start to strategize and think about the resources available to us, if we study history, and if we look at Jesus's model, we'll realize young adults are the ones who will revolutionize the world.

Another Great Awakening

By the way, has God ever captured America's attention and turned it back to him? Yes. Ever heard the term "Great Awakening" in your history books? You might also call these revivals. Some experts would say we've had four in our nation's history. I've looked at these events, studying them and charting them out. It's interesting—they've happened roughly every fifty years. How crazy is that? The first Great Awakening was in 1720, and the last one ended in the late 1960s. Just over fifty years ago. Based on this rhythm, we could be poised for another Great Awakening soon.

And that's not all. Let's say God does work in this rhythm, though he's certainly not obligated to or bound to it. But let's just say he was going to start another Great Awakening. Who would he use? Young adults have been at the epicenter of all the previous Great Awakenings. The first one was led by Jonathan Edwards and George Whitefield, who were both in their twenties. The second one was led by Lyman Beecher and Peter Cartwright, who were also twentysomething at the time. The third was largely led by D. L. Moody, who was in his early twenties, and Ira D. Sankey, who was in his early thirties. And the fourth Great Awakening (though this one is more debated) was led significantly by Billy Graham while he was in his twenties and early thirties. Young adults have been at the center of every significant spiritual revival in our country.

Here's what that means for you: the greatest opportunity for you to change the world for Jesus Christ is for you to take whatever days you have left and invest them in reaching young adults. Study and learn about this generation and the ones that follow. Spend your time with them. Teach them the things Jesus has taught you. Disciple them. And call them to something great—because they are the future of the church. Without young adults, your church has no future. But with them, and with the King of heaven moving in the hearts of his people, not even the gates of hell will be able to stop you from advancing the gospel (Matt. 16:18). Let's go, church!

Acknowledgments

So much of what I know about ministry I've learned from my friend and mentor Todd Wagner. He has modeled what it looks like to care about and invest in the future of the church. Watermark and The Porch are doing so much to reach the future of the church. Watch them and learn from them, as I continue to.

My friend and ministry partner Luke Friesen did an incredible work of capturing the right ministry stories to share in this book. I am thankful for his unique skills that have made The Porch better and this book possible. Also, Greg Crooks went before Luke and has long been an incredible ministry partner to me. I would not still be in ministry if not for these men and their patience and grace toward me.

David Marvin and I have been at war together, fighting evil and training up the future of the church. I am thankful for his friendship and partnership in the gospel.

My wife, Monica, is the best ministry partner anyone could ask for. She put the kids to bed without me every Tuesday night for over a decade while I was preaching at The Porch. She is truly the kindest person I know. Together, we seek to reach and develop the future of the church.

Lastly, the people and staff of Harris Creek, where I now pastor, have welcomed us with open arms. At Harris Creek, we get to influence college students at Baylor and send them around the world. Our family is so excited about the mission before us, and I'm thankful that God has created a place for us to lead here in Waco, Texas.

Notes

Introduction The World's Most Influential Generation

1. "You've Gotta Love Millennials—Micah Tyler," YouTube video, 2:57, posted April 30, 2016, https://www.youtube.com/watch?v=hLpE1Pa8vvI.

2. For more information about Watermark's annual Church Leaders Conference, see www.churchleadersconference.com.

3. Jonathan Pokluda, "'Generation Why?' Statistics," *The Porch* (blog), October 15, 2012, https://www.theporch.live/blogs/generation-why-statistics.

4. Pokluda, "'Generation Why?' Statistics."

Chapter 1 Be Real

1. You can watch this moment for yourself, starting around the 43:14 mark. Jonathan Pokluda, "Romans 8:5–13: Choose God to Be in the Driver's Seat," Watermark, March 29, 2016, www.watermark.org/message/3976.

2. Watermark Community Church, "Values," Watermark, accessed December 15, 2017, www.watermark.org/about/beliefs/values.

Chapter 2 Teach the Whole Truth

1. Jonathan Pokluda and David Marvin, "Dating Decisions," The Porch, accessed April 22, 2018, http://www.theporch.live/messages/2581.

2. Bob Smietana, "Americans Love God and the Bible, Are Fuzzy on the Details," LifeWay Research, September 27, 2016, https://lifewayresearch.com/2016/09/27/americans-love-god-and-the-bible-are-fuzzy-on-the-details/.

3. Pew Research Center, "Religious Composition of Younger Millennials," *Pew Forum*, accessed April 21, 2018, http://www.pewforum.org/religious-landscape-study/generational-cohort/younger-millennial/.

4. R. Albert Mohler Jr., "Moralistic Therapeutic Deism—the New American Religion," *CP Opinion*, April 18, 2005, https://www.christianpost.com/news/moralistic-therapeutic-deism-the-new-american-religion-6266/.

5. Barna Group, "The Bible in America: 6-Year Trends," Barna, June 15, 2016, https://www.barna.com/research/the-bible-in-america-6-year-trends/.

6. Lydia Saad, "Record Few Americans Believe Bible Is Literal Word of God," *Gallup*, May 15, 2017, https://news.gallup.com/poll/210704/record-few-americans-believe-bible-literal-word-god.aspx.

7. "21 Books You Don't Have to Read," *GQ*, April 19, 2018, https://www.gq.com/story/21-books-you-dont-have-to-read.

8. Barna Group, "State of the Bible 2017: Top Findings," Barna, April 4, 2017, https://www.barna.com/research/state-bible-2017-top-findings/.

9. Sarah Zylstra, "What the Latest Bible Research Reveals about Millennials," *Christianity Today*, May 16, 2016, https://www.christianitytoday.com/news/2016/may/what-latest-bible-research-reveals-about-millennials.html.

10. Sarah Zylstra, "'Do Not Be Discouraged': YouVersion Bible App Tops 300 Million Downloads," *Christianity Today*, January 3, 2018, https://www.christianitytoday.com/news/2018/january/youversion-bible-app-2017-top-verses-downloads.html.

11. Lillian Kwon, "Biblical Illiteracy in US at Crisis Point, Says Bible Expert," *Christian Post*, June 16, 2014, https://www.christianpost.com/news/biblical-illiteracy-in-us-at-crisis-point-says-bible-expert-121626/.

12. Ellen Byron, "America's Retailers Have a New Target Customer: The 26-Year-Old Millennial," *Wall Street Journal*, October 9, 2017, https://www.wsj.com/articles/americas-retailers-have-a-new-target-customer-the-26-year-old-millennial-1507559181.

13. Barna Group, "5 Ways to Connect with Millennials," Barna, September 9, 2014, https://www.barna.com/research/5-ways-to-connect-with-millennials/.

14. Travis Bradberry, "How Complaining Rewires Your Brain for Negativity," Talentsmart, accessed April 5, 2018, http://www.talentsmart.com/articles/How-Complaining-Rewires-Your-Brain-for-Negativity-2147446676-p-1.html.

15. Purdue University, "Money Only Buys Happiness for a Certain Amount: Research Looks at How Much Money Makes Individuals around the World Happy," *ScienceDaily*, February 13, 2018, www.sciencedaily.com/releases/2018/02/180213132926.htm.

16. David DiSalvo, "Generosity Boosts Well-Being by Tuning Down the Brain's Anxiety Center, Research Suggests," *Forbes*, September 10, 2018, https://www.forbes.com/sites/daviddisalvo/2018/09/10/generosity-isnt-just-about-doing-good-its-also-good-for-our-mental-health-suggests-new-study/#3e125a095286.

17. Dave Heller, "Lead Us Not into Temptation: Predictors for Infidelity, Divorce Highlighted in New FSU Research," *Florida State University News*, February 12, 2018, https://news.fsu.edu/news/education-society/2018/02/12/lead-us-not-temptation-predictors-infidelity-divorce-highlighted-new-fsu-research/.

18. Scott Stanley, "Premarital Cohabitation Is Still Associated with Greater Odds of Divorce," Institute for Family Studies, October 17, 2018, https://ifst udies.org/blog/premarital-cohabitation-is-still-associated-with-greater-odds -of-divorce.

19. "Forgiveness: Your Health Depends on It," Johns Hopkins Medicine, accessed October 13, 2018, https://www.hopkinsmedicine.org/health/healthy _aging/healthy_connections/forgiveness-your-health-depends-on-it.

20. Alice Walton, "People in the U.S. Are Drinking More Alcohol Than Ever: Study," *Forbes*, August 12, 2017, https://www.forbes.com/sites/aliceg walton/2017/08/12/people-in-the-u-s-are-drinking-more-alcohol-than-ever -study/#18dad8e43eb7.

21. Leigh Weingus, "What Does Sober Curious Mean? Here's Why You're Seeing That Term So Much Lately," *Bustle*, October 11, 2018, https://www.bustle .com/p/what-does-sober-curious-mean-heres-why-youre-seeing-that-term -so-much-lately-12017945.

22. Ashitha Nagesh, "Forget Hygge, Let's All Get Päntsdrunk," *BBC*, June 6, 2018, https://www.bbc.co.uk/bbcthree/article/8c1960fc-5a7f-4f4a-9e82 -d9e774c4ee5a.

23. You can also find these messages on The Porch app on iTunes / Google Play.

24. Visit The Porch message archives at https://www.theporch.live/mes sages.

25. Visit *The Porch* (blog) at http://www.theporch.live/blogs.

Chapter 3 Get Good Feedback

1. Ross Blankenship, "How the Most Effective Managers Give Feedback," *Forbes*, October 21, 2016, https://www.forbes.com/sites/forbescoachescou ncil/2016/10/21/how-the-most-effective-managers-give-feedback/#3b614c 8b546b.

2. Wes Gay, "The Worst Way to Engage Millennials with Feedback and How to Avoid It," *Forbes*, January 9, 2017, https://www.forbes.com/sites/wesg ay/2017/01/09/the-worst-way-to-engage-millennials-with-feedback-and-how -to-avoid-it/#7e5f8bbe6e1e.

3. Jim Harter and Amy Adkins, "Employees Want a Lot More from Their Managers," *Gallup*, April 8, 2015, http://news.gallup.com/businessjournal/18 2321/employees-lot-managers.aspx.

4. Christine Porath, "Give Your Team More-Effective Positive Feedback," *Harvard Business Review*, October 25, 2016, https://hbr.org/2016/10/give-your -team-more-effective-positive-feedback.

Chapter 4 Hold Traditions Loosely

1. Jaroslav Pelikan, *The Vindication of Tradition: The 1983 Jefferson Lecture in the Humanities* (New Haven: Yale University Press, 1986), 65.

2. Thom Rainer, "13 Issues for Churches in 2013," *ChurchLeaders*, January 15, 2013, https://churchleaders.com/pastors/pastor-articles/164787-thom-rainer-13-issues-churches-2013.html.

3. US Census Data, "Historical Marital Status Tables: November 2018," United States Census Bureau, accessed May 10, 2018, https://www.census.gov/data/tables/time-series/demo/families/marital.html.

4. John Fleming, "Gallup Analysis: Millennials, Marriage, and Family," *Gallup*, May 19, 2016, http://news.gallup.com/poll/191462/gallup-analysis-millennials-marriage-family.aspx.

5. Jonathan Pokluda, "10 Things a Man Should Look for in a Woman," *The Porch* (blog), October 2, 2017, http://www.theporch.live/blogs/10-things-a-man-should-look-for-in-a-woman/; Pokluda, "10 Things a Woman Should Look for in a Man," *The Porch* (blog), September 25, 2017, http://www.theporch.live/blogs/10-things-a-woman-should-look-for-in-a-man.

6. "Save the Date," The Porch, accessed August 22, 2019, http://www.theporch.live/messages/3543; Jonathan Pokluda, "How Do I Know If I Have the Gift of Singleness?" *The Porch* (blog), November 16, 2015, http://www.theporch.live/blogs/gift-of-singleness/.

7. Barna Group, "What Millennials Want When They Visit Church," Barna, March 4, 2015, https://www.barna.com/research/what-millennials-want-when-they-visit-church/.

8. Barna Group, "What Millennials Want When They Visit Church."

9. LifeWay Staff, "Have a Mentor; Be a Mentor—The Biblical Model of Mentoring," LifeWay, January 1, 2014, https://www.lifeway.com/en/articles/biblical-model-of-mentoring.

Chapter 5 Under-Promise and Over-Deliver

1. Lauren Friedman, "Millennials and the Digital Experience: Getting Your Digital Act Together," *Forbes*, February 8, 2017, https://www.forbes.com/sites/laurenfriedman/2017/02/08/millennials-and-the-digital-experience-getting-your-digital-act-together/#5e2d741c730d.

2. Or "Fear of Missing Out," for those unfamiliar with the acronym.

Chapter 6 Define a Path Forward

1. Jeremiah Jensen, "Study: Millennials Wrestle with the American Dream of Homeownership," *HousingWire*, July 23, 2018, https://www.housingwire.com/articles/46144-study-millennials-wrestle-with-the-american-dream-of-homeownership.

2. "Should I? Making Wise Choices," Watermark, accessed September 18, 2019, https://www.watermark.org/series/323.

3. Julia Glum, "53% of Millennials Expect to Become Millionaires One Day, according to a New Study," *Time*, June 11, 2018, http://time.com/money/5308043/millennials-millionaires-new-research/.

4. Raul Hernandez, "Millennials Owe a Record Amount of Debt, and It Could Become a Huge Drag on the Economy," *Business Insider,* April 29, 2017, https://www.businessinsider.com/record-millennial-debt-a-drag-on-the-economy-2017-4.

5. Emily Sullivan, "Why Aren't Millennials Spending? They're Poorer Than Previous Generations, Fed Says," *NPR,* November 30, 2018, https://www.npr.org/2018/11/30/672103209/why-arent-millennials-spending-more-they-re-poorer-than-their-parents-fed-says.

6. Pokluda, "How Do I Know If I Have the Gift of Singleness?"

7. Jonathan Pokluda, "10 Things to Do While You're Single," *The Porch* (blog), July 17, 2017, http://www.theporch.live/blogs/10-things-to-do-while-youre-single.

8. Jonathan Pokluda, "5 Reasons Why Marriage Is Better Than Singleness (and Vice Versa)," *The Porch* (blog), June 15, 2014, https://www.theporch.live/blogs/5-reasons-why-marriage-is-better-than-singleness-and-vice-versa; Pokluda, "5 Reasons Why Singleness Is Better Than Marriage (and Vice Versa)," *The Porch* (blog), June 15, 2014, https://www.theporch.live/blogs/5-reasons-why-singleness-is-better-than-marriage-and-vice-versa.

9. Caroline Beaton, "Why Millennials Are Lonely," *Forbes,* February 9, 2017, https://www.forbes.com/sites/carolinebeaton/2017/02/09/why-millennials-are-lonely/#3999541d7c35.

10. Ronald C. Kessler et al., "The Global Burden of Mental Disorders: An Update from the WHO World Mental Health (WMH) Surveys," *Epidemiol Psichiatr Soc.* 18, no. 1 (2009): 23–33, https://www.ncbi.nlm.nih.gov/pubmed/19378696.

11. Norman B. Anderson et al., "Stress in America: Paying with Our Health," American Psychological Association, February 4, 2015, https://www.apa.org/news/press/releases/stress/2014/stress-report.pdf.

12. I know that sounds simple . . . maybe even too simple. But I believe it's true. Anxiety can be a complicated topic, and lots of Scriptures speak into it. I address the topic much more fully in *Welcome to Adulting.*

13. Roxy Stone and David Kinnaman, "When Millennials Go to Work," Barna, June 9, 2016, https://www.barna.com/research/when-millennials-go-to-work/.

14. Stone and Kinnaman, "When Millennials Go to Work."

15. "Singles in America," Match, accessed August 22, 2019, https://www.singlesinamerica.com/2018/#SINGLESINAMERICA.

16. Jonathan Pokluda, "How to Be a Godly Woman," *The Porch* (blog), April 20, 2015, https://www.theporch.live/blogs/how-to-be-a-godly-woman/; Jonathan Pokluda, "How to Be a Man," *The Porch* (blog), March 23, 2015, https://www.theporch.live/blogs/how-to-be-a-man/.

17. Pokluda, "10 Things a Man Should Look for in a Woman."

18. Pokluda, "10 Things a Woman Should Look for in a Man."

19. Jonathan Pokluda, "Dating 101: The Ask," *The Porch* (blog), July 2, 2012, https://www.theporch.live/blogs/dating-101-the-ask/.

20. Jonathan Pokluda, "Get Married Already," *The Porch* (blog), June 8, 2015, https://www.theporch.live/blogs/get-married-already/.

21. Don't believe me? Let's do the math. After 2 years, there would only be 9 people changed—yourself, the 2 you discipled the first year, and the 6 people that you and your 2 friends discipled the second year. The next year those 9 people would add 18 more, for a total of 27. After 5 years, there would be a total of 243 people changed. In 10 years, the number would be just over 59,000. In 20 years, you will reach almost 3.5 billion. And sometime in the 21st year you will have reached every single person on the planet.

Chapter 7 Find Leaders

1. I've changed the names of the heroes in these true stories, but they know who they are.
2. "The Life Initiative," Watermark, accessed September 18, 2019, http:// www.watermark.org/dallas/ministries/tli.
3. Stone and Kinnaman, "When Millennials Go to Work."
4. "How Millennials Want to Work and Live," *Gallup*, accessed February 1, 2018, http://news.gallup.com/reports/189830/millennials-work-live.aspx.
5. "Watermark Covenant," Watermark, accessed August 26, 2019, www .watermark.org/covenant.
6. "Conflict Field Guide," Watermark, accessed August 26, 2019, http://www .watermark.org/dallas/ministries/community/resources/conflict-field-guide.
7. Business Dictionary, s.v. "Peter Principle," *Business Dictionary*, accessed February 12, 2018, http://www.businessdictionary.com/definition/Peter -principle.html.

Chapter 8 Call Them to Greatness

1. Luke 9:23–24.
2. Got Questions Ministries, "What Is the Romans Road to Salvation?" GotQuestions, accessed December 15, 2017, https://www.gotquestions.org /Romans-road-salvation.html.
3. You can find the application and commitment to serve with The Porch at: http://www.theporch.live/connect#ServewithUs.
4. Pol Pinoy, "American Psychiatric Association Makes It Official: 'Selfie' a Mental Disorder," *Adobo Chronicles*, March 31, 2014, https://adobochronicl es.com/2014/03/31/american-psychiatric-association-makes-it-official-selfie -a-mental-disorder/.
5. Janarthanan Balakrishnan and Mark Griffiths, "An Exploratory Study of Selfitis and the Development of the Selfitis Behavior Scale," *International Journal of Mental Health and Addiction* 16, no. 3 (June 2018): 722–36, https:// link.springer.com/article/10.1007%2Fs11469-017-9844-x.
6. AAFPRS, "Social Media Makes Lasting Impact on Industry—Becomes Cultural Force, Not Fad," American Academy of Facial Plastic and Reconstructive Surgery, January 23, 2019, https://www.aafprs.org/media/stats_polls/m _stats.html.

7. Katie Silver, "Adolescence Now Lasts from 10 to 24," *BBC News*, January 19, 2018, http://www.bbc.com/news/health-42732442.

8. Jonathan Pokluda, "How to Be Great," *The Porch* (blog), June 2, 2014, https://www.theporch.live/blogs/how-to-be-great/.

9. Jonathan Pokluda, "How Will You Be Remembered? You Won't," *The Porch* (blog), May 28, 2018, https://www.theporch.live/blogs/how-will-you -be-remembered/.

10. Jonathan Pokluda, "The Greatest Sin," *The Porch* (blog), November 27, 2017, https://www.theporch.live/blogs/the-greatest-sin/.

11. Jonathan Pokluda, "Revolutionary Humility," *The Porch* (blog), February 13, 2017, https://www.theporch.live/blogs/revolutionary-humility/.

Chapter 9 Give the Ministry Away

1. "Unashamed," Watermark, accessed August 26, 2019, www.unashamed network.org.

2. "Ministries," Watermark, accessed August 26, 2019, http://www.water mark.org/ministries.

3. Jonathan Pokluda, "How to Know if You've Found 'The One,'" *The Porch* (blog), October 23, 2017, http://www.theporch.live/blogs/how-to-know-if -youve-found-the-one/.

4. Jonathan Pokluda, "How to Tell Your Story: 10 Tips," *The Porch* (blog), April 29, 2013, http://www.theporch.live/blogs/how-to-tell-your-story-10-tips/.

5. Jonathan Pokluda, "How to Find and Use Your Gifts," *The Porch* (blog), August 24, 2015, http://www.theporch.live/blogs/how-to-find-and-use-your-gifts/.

Chapter 10 Create Unique Shared Experiences

1. These are all in good fun. No one is forced to play who doesn't want to, and anyone is welcome to lobby for an alternate consequence before they decide to jump in the game. But once the consequence is set and you choose to join in, you're committed to do it if you lose!

2. And yes, we gave the ring back to the store.

3. This was definitely not a real protest—Genesis 9:3 had a lot of support among Porch staff. Thankfully no one was stabbed in the making of that video.

4. We paid for replacements afterward.

5. Chad Brooks, "Why Your Employees Hate Teamwork," *Business News Daily*, December 9, 2016, https://www.businessnewsdaily.com/9616-employees -hate-teamwork.html.

6. "Google Search Statistics," *Internet Live Stats*, accessed August 7, 2018, http://www.internetlivestats.com/google-search-statistics/.

7. Charles Duhig, "What Google Learned from Its Quest to Build the Perfect Team," *New York Times*, February 25, 2016, https://www.nytimes.com/20 16/02/28/magazine/what-google-learned-from-its-quest-to-build-the-perfect -team.html?_r=3.

8. Jeffrey Kranz, "All the 'One Another' Commands in the NT," *Overview Bible*, March 9, 2014, https://overviewbible.com/one-another-infographic/.

9. Kyle also encouraged everyone to spend time studying Exodus 18:17–26, which has formed the foundation of his approach to team building.

10. Erica Boothby and Margaret Clark, "Shared Experiences Are Amplified," *Psychological Science*, October 1, 2014, http://journals.sagepub.com/doi/abs/10.1177/0956797614551162.

11. August Giacoman, "The Serious Fun of Shared Experiences at Work," *Strategy+Business*, November 7, 2016, https://www.strategy-business.com/blog/The-Serious-Fun-of-Shared-Experiences-at-Work?gko=56576.

12. Giacoman, "The Serious Fun of Shared Experiences at Work."

13. I'll let you in on a little secret: I'm not actually obsessed with Farkle (though it may seem like it). But I am obsessed with what Farkle *does*—creates a near-guaranteed shared experience and fun memory. You could pick any other game or activity that does the same thing, and make it your own.

Chapter 11 Remember the Vision

1. Richard R. Thomas, "From Porch to Patio," *The Palimpsest*, accessed November 2, 2018, https://www.frontporchrepublic.com/wp-content/uploads/2009/03/From-Porch-to-Patio-R.-Thomas.pdf.

2. Jamie Ducharme, "Young Americans Are the Loneliest, according to a New Study," *Time*, May 1, 2018, http://time.com/5261181/young-americans-are-lonely/.

3. "Trulia: 1 in 2 Americans Don't Know Neighbors' Names," *Forbes*, October 24, 2013, https://www.forbes.com/sites/trulia/2013/10/24/neighbor-survey/#336e418c616e.

4. Michael Lipka, "Major U.S. Metropolitan Areas Differ in their Religious Profiles," Pew Research Center, July 29, 2015, http://www.pewresearch.org/fact-tank/2015/07/29/major-u-s-metropolitan-areas-differ-in-their-religious-profiles/.

5. Caitlin McCormack, "The 5 Most Surprisingly Dangerous Big Cities in America," Safety, April 15, 2019, https://www.safety.com/dangerous-cities/#gref.

6. Ryan Osborne, "Dallas Sins Harder Than New Orleans? New List Puts Our Vanity and Lust among the Best," WFAA-8, November 27, 2018, https://www.wfaa.com/article/news/dallas-sins-harder-than-new-orleans-new-list-puts-our-vanity-and-lust-among-the-best/287-618055904.

Conclusion Starting a Revolution

1. "Napoleon Biography," Biography, August 1, 2019, https://www.biography.com/people/napoleon-9420291.

2. Todd Andrlik, "Ages of Revolution: How Old Were They on July 4, 1776?" *Journal of the American Revolution*, August 8, 2013, https://allthingsliberty.com/2013/08/ages-of-revolution-how-old-1776/.

3. "Hugh Hefner Biography," Biography, April 15, 2019, https://www.biography.com/people/hugh-hefner-9333521.

About the Authors

Jonathan "JP" Pokluda is the lead pastor of Harris Creek Baptist Church in Waco, Texas. He was formerly the leader of The Porch and a teaching pastor of Watermark Community Church in Dallas. Under his leadership, The Porch grew to be the largest young adult ministry of its kind in the world.

JP came to understand the grace of the gospel in his early twenties after being involved in different denominational churches his entire life. This ignited a desire in him to inspire young adults to radically follow Jesus Christ and unleash them to change the world. Most recently, he has seen this passion come out through writing. His bestselling book, *Welcome to Adulting*, offers Millennials a road map to navigating faith, finances, friendships, and the future. He spends his spare time consulting with churches and helping them reach the next generation.

JP's partner in ministry is his wife of fifteen years, Monica, and together they have fun discipling their children, Presley, Finley, and Weston.

Luke Friesen is director of operations at Watermark Community Church. He has been involved with The Porch for more than ten years as a staff member, volunteer, and attendee. As an editor and contributor to *The Porch* blog, he's collaborated with JP on a number of writing projects. He and his wife, Chelsea, have one daughter, Winslett.

Also Available from
JP POKLUDA

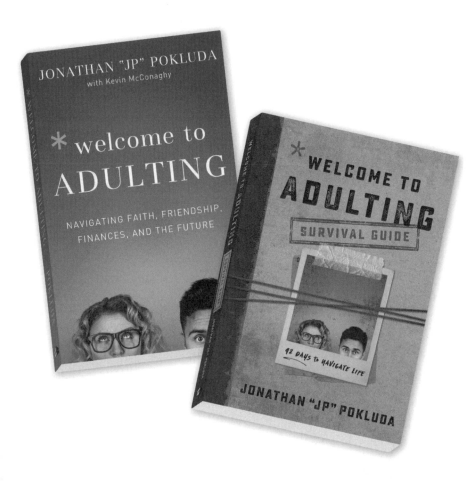

Adulting is hard. Luckily, these go-to guides help answer all of your "now what?" questions about adult life.

JONATHAN POKLUDA

CONNECT WITH JP

 Jonathan Pokluda | JPokluda | JPokluda

Dear Leader of Future Leaders,

First, I am so encouraged that you would pick up this resource and see it as a worthwhile investment of time. I have had the privilege of watching God move in a generation, and in doing so, I've become completely convinced of how important it is to reach and teach the future of our churches. As I've said in this book, "If we are not reaching the future of the church, our church has no future." I am thankful you take that calling seriously. Know that I pray for leaders like you often, and if I can help you in your mission, I want to. You can follow me through these platforms as you and I follow Jesus together.

Do not grow weary in your mission of reaching the future. Keep going!

Sincerely,

Jonathan Pokluda

Harris Creek

Available in App Stores